Modern Collectible Dolls

IDENTIFICATION & VALUE GUIDE

VOLUME III

Patsy Moyer

COLLECTOR BOOKS
A Division of Schroeder Publishing Co., Inc.

The current values in this book should be used only as a guide. They are not intended to set prices, which vary from one section of the country to another. Auction prices as well as dealer prices vary greatly and are affected by condition as well as demand. Neither the author nor the publisher assumes responsibility for any losses that might be incurred as a result of consulting this guide.

Searching for a Publisher?

We are always looking for knowledgeable people considered to be experts within their fields. If you feel that there is a real need for a book on your collectible subject and have a large comprehensive collection, contact Collector Books.

On the Cover:
Front:
Left:
14" composition Arranbee (R&B) Nancy Lee, all original in blue organdy, cotton slip, attached panties, with hang tag, sleep eyes, mohair wig, beautiful color, circa 1936 – 1938, $450.00. Courtesy Peggy Millhouse.
Right top:
9" painted hard plastic Baitz Tegernsee girl, painted features, mohair wig, side-glancing eyes, round open/closed mouth, felt over wire body, original regional outfit, Baitz heart tag, sticker *Made in Austria,* circa 1970s, $75.00. Private collection.
Right middle:
10" English composition Old Cottage Toys Tweedle Dee and Tweedle Dum, circa 1968, all original, $625.00 pair. Courtesy Dorothy Bohlin.
Right bottom:
17½" felt Lenci Tyrolean Girl, 300 Series, shows intricate costuming company is famous for, pierced ears with earrings are rare on Lencis, circa 1929, $2,000.00. Courtesy Nancy Lazenby.

Back:
Left:
21" porcelain artist doll Allexis by Linda Lee Sutton Originals, porcelain limbs, issued in 1995, limited edition of 10, $595.00. Courtesy Linda Lee Sutton.
Middle:
20" vinyl American Character Toni, all original high heeled doll with bag of accessories, $475.00. Courtesy June Algeier.
Right:
19" vinyl Heidi Ott Serina #2.84, with human hair wig, brown eyes, cloth body, red dress with pinafore, circa 1984, $300.00. Courtesy Linda Maddux.

Cover design: Beth Summers
Book design: Holly C. Long

COLLECTOR BOOKS
P.O. Box 3009
Paducah, Kentucky 42002–3009

Copyright © 1999 by Patsy Moyer

Printed in the U.S.A. by Image Graphics, Paducah, KY

Contents

Dedication

Every woman, especially doll collectors, should have a daughter. My own precious little jewel was born November 11, 1956, and was immediately nicknamed my own "Living Doll." Girls are so much fun; you automatically relate to them and it is especially nice when they like dolls. I was lucky enough to have one daughter, Marilyn Marie Moyer Ramsey and I am especially proud of her as a daughter, a mother, a wife, and a very strong, courageous young woman who has achieved many goals.

Credits

Algeier, June
Atkinson, Cleveland
Baca, Connie
Barckley, Jo
Baskins, Bonnie
Baylis, Stella Mae
Beston, Micki
Bennett, Carol
Bohlin, Dorothy
Bolli, Lisa
Booth, Lilian
Boucher, Vivian
Brown, Ruth
Burklen, Sandra
Busch, Millie
Callens, Teddy
Carol, Millie
Cermak, Dee
Chase, Susan
Chesnut, Cathy
Clark, Cathie
Colan, Joann
Cook, Irma
Crosby, Betty
Crume, Debbie
Cunha, Helga
Davis, Debby
DeFeo, Barbara
DeMattei, Kay
DeSmet, Sally
Elliot, Nancy
Emmerson, Marie
Eshom, Shirley

Fabian, Frances
Fairchild, Carol
Fetsco, Suzanne
Foote, Darlene
Foster, Jane
Fronefield, Betty Jane
Franz, Mary Jane
Fronk, Vickie
Fudge, Mary
Gallagher, Faye Newberry
Gervais, Cherie
Gonzales, Angie
Graf, Mary Evelyn
Graves, Diane
Gregg, Odis
Grundtvig, Irene
Guss, Judith
Hadley, Donna
Hash, Amanda
Hill, Janet
Hilliker, Barbara
Hogh, Jeanie
Holton, Linda
Horst, Jane
Hustler, Penny
Jacobs, Jennine
Jackson, Maxine
Jenness, Diana
Jeschien, Chantal
Jesurun, Delores L.
Jones, Ana Maria
Jones, Iva Mae
Jueden, Jaci

Kinkade, Sue
Klenke, Rae
Kolibaba, Sharon
Krueger, Sondra
LaRusso, Michael
Lazenby, Nancy
Lotz, Jean
Lyon, Pauline
Maddux, Linda
Martin, Connie Lee
Martinec, Pam
Mata, Olivina
McMasters Doll Auctions
McMorran, Jill
McWilliams, Christine
Meade, Shirley
Meisinger, Marge
Mertz, Ursula
Metz, Martha
Millhouse, Peggy
Mitchell, Bev
Mock, Arthur
Morgan, Joanne
Montgomery, Marcie
Olivo, Susan Martin
Ortega, Dolores
Osborn, Dorisanne
Perez-Daple, Lourdes
Pettygrove, Marian
Pittsley, Penny
Prince, Stephanie
Quigley, Rachel R.
Rich, Nancy

Robertson, Sue
Rodgers, Marie
Rose, Lori
Sanders, Jill
Santacruce, Janet
Saunders, Mary Lynne
Schuda, Pat
Shall, David
Shelton, Brenda
Shelton, Kim
Shelton, Nelda
Shirran, Sherryl
Shupe, Catherine
Smedes, Gay
Smith, Kathy and Roy
Sturgess, Ellen
Surber, Elizabeth
Sutton, Linda Lee
Swalwell, Ruth
Tannenbaum, Leslie
Thompson, Amy
Thompson, Jean
Travis, Annmarie
Trowbridge, Mary Lu
Victoriano, Espy
Viskocil, Peggy
Vitale, Kim
Wetenkamp, Sheryl
Williams, Louise
Wolbers, Kathryn
Yadon, Bette

Introduction

So you want to be a doll collector. Where, then, shall you begin? Whatever reason motivates you — perhaps it is nostalgia for your childhood dolls or the enjoyment of the doll as an art form. Or perhaps it is the need to nurture something that reminds you of a child, the urge to create costumes or the chance to escape the reality of the sometimes harsh day-to-day world. Doll collecting is a wonderful hobby to enjoy; and for the novice collector, knowledge is power.

You need that knowledge to get the best for your money. Unless you have won the lottery or made a million in software or the stock market, you probably have a limited budget. Those of us who are not independently wealthy need to know that we are spending our money wisely — so that when the time comes for us to part with our collection, it will have increased in value. Thus your next doll might be considered a portable asset.

As a novice collector you need to learn as much about doll collecting and your chosen niche as possible. This means you need to see a large number of dolls so that you can tell the good from the bad. You need to find out as much about your next doll as possible to know that you got a good buy. This book is a showcase of dolls that collectors have acquired. It will help you find an example of a certain costume and gives examples of how older dolls may look now.

Perhaps *modern* is a misnomer for dolls over 70 years old. However, some doll companies that made dolls at the turn of the century are still operating and producing today. For this book, I am grouping as modern, dolls made of composition, cloth, rubber, hard plastic, porcelain, vinyl, wood, and some other materials, as opposed to dolls of bisque, wax, wood, and china that were made before World War I. There are no easy cut-off dates and some spill over from one category to the next. This book will give you examples of dolls to compare for identification.

Collectors who want to know more about the dolls they have or want to collect, need to learn as much as possible. One way to do this is to research and arm yourself with books and magazines that deal with the subject. Another way is to seek other informed collectors. Beginning collectors should list their dolls with the prices paid, the size, marks, material, and other pertinent facts, such as originality and condition. Collectors need to be able to identify their dolls and one way to do this is by material.

Experienced doll collectors refer to a doll by whatever material is used for making the doll's head. So a composition doll has a composition head but may have a cloth, composition, or wood body. A doll with a vinyl head and a hard plastic body is a vinyl doll. The head commands the order of reference to the doll in relation to materials used to produce it. A doll made entirely of vinyl is referred to as all-vinyl.

It is nice when exact measurements are given to describe the height of the doll.

To identify a doll with no packaging or box, first examine the back of the head, then the torso, and the rest of the body, the usual places manufacturers put their marks. Some dolls will only have a mold number or no mark at all. Nursing students are often given the task of writing a physical description of their patient starting at the top of their head down to the bottom of their feet. This is also a good way of describing a doll and its attire.

Collectors like to meet and speak with other collectors who share their interests. For this reason we have included a Collectors' Network section in the back of this book. There are many special interest groups focusing on one area of doll collecting. These are experienced collectors who will consult with others. It is considered proper form to send a SASE when contacting others if you wish to receive a reply. If you wish to be included in this area, please send your area of expertise and references.

In addition, a national organization, the United Federation of Doll Clubs has information for doll collectors who are seeking, or wish to form, a doll club. The goals of this nonprofit organization focus on education, research, preservation, and enjoyment of dolls. They also sponsor a Junior Membership for budding doll collectors. They will put you in contact with one of 16 regional directors who will be able to assess your needs and advise you if a doll club in your area is accepting members. You may write for more information to UFDC, 10920 North Ambassador Drive, Suite 130, Kansas City, MO 64153, or fax 816 891-8360.

Beginning collectors will want to learn as much as possible about dolls before spending their money. It seems prudent to investigate thoroughly all avenues regarding an addition to one's collection before actually making a purchase.

Novice collectors may wonder where to buy dolls. There are many different ways to find the doll of your dreams, including dealers or shops that will locate a particular doll for you. There are numerous focus groups that list special sales. Collector groups usually post doll shows and sales in their newsletters.

Auctions may also prove to be an aid in finding additions to your collection. Some offer absentee bidding which is most helpful if you do not live near. Some also offer phone bidding if you want to be in on the actual bidding. Auction houses usually send out catalogs and are most helpful in answering questions over the phone or fax. See Collectors' Network at the back of this book for more information.

All of the more usual sources may pale in comparison with the mushrooming effect of the Internet. Type in "dolls" in one of the search engines and you will get hundreds of thousands of responses. Trying to navigate the "Net" and finding what you are looking for is a daunting task made easier by some of our sources. And with auctions, like ebay which specialize in dolls, as well as many other collectibles, it can easily overwhelm the budding collector. You will need research to quickly know the attributes of desirable dolls so you can make decisions on whether to buy.

Not only are books, magazines, and videos available for collectors, but simply going to museums, doll shows, and displays is a wonderful way for the collector to see dolls. To help the novice collector, simple tips on what to look for in dolls are included in this book.

Just as the most valuable quality in real estate is location, location, location; a doll collector should consider condition, condition, condition. Dolls with good color, original clothing, tags, brochures, and boxes will always be desirable. The trick is to find those dolls that also have rarity, beauty, or some other unique quality that makes them appealing to the collector. It could be that only a few were made. It could be that a collector recalls his/her childhood dolls. Or it could be that a doll's manufacture, presentation, or identity make a historical statement. Other factors can also contribute to the desirability and popularity of a doll. Cleanliness, good color, and good condition are always desirable qualities.

An easy way to keep track of the money spent on doll collections is to utilize a money program on your computer, using a number and description to keep track of your doll, then entering the amount you spent. If you sell the doll or dispose of it, the doll can be checked during the reconciling procedure and will not be seen on your current inventory. This is just a very simple way to help you with your doll inventory.

This book does not mean to set prices and should only be used as one of many tools to guide the collector. It is the collector's decision alone on which doll to purchase. It is the responsibility of the collector alone to choose his or her own area of collecting and how to pursue it. This book is meant to help you enjoy and learn about dolls of our past and present and give indications of future trends. If you wish to see other categories or wish to share your collection, please write to the address in Collectors' Network in the back of the book.

Happy collecting!

Advertising Dolls

Companies often use dolls as a means of advertising their products, either as a premium or in the form of a trademark of their company. This entrepreneurial spirit has given us some delightful examples. Not meant primarily as a collectible, but as a means to promote products or services, the advertising doll has been around since the late 1800s, and continues to be a viable form of advertising. Advertising dolls now can be made just for the collector — look at the Christmas ornaments that advertise Barbie, space adventurers, and the McDonald's restaurant premiums in their Happy Meal boxes. All of these dolls or figurines that promote a product or service are called advertising dolls. Early companies that used dolls to promote their products were Amberg with Vanta Baby, American Cereal Co. with Cereta, American Character with the Campbell Kids, Buster Brown Shoes with Buster Brown, Ideal with Cracker Jack Boy and ZuZu Kid, Kellogg's with a variety of characters, and many others.

What to look for:

This is a wonderful field for collectors as you may find dolls others overlook. Dolls can be of any material, but those mint-in-box or with original advertising will remain the most desirable. Cloth should have bright colors, no tears, little soil, and retain printed identifying marks. On dolls of other materials, look for rosy cheeks, little wear, cleanliness, and originality, original tags, labels, boxes, or brochures. Keep dates and purchasing information when you obtain current products. This information will add to the value of your collectibles.

17" foam rubber The Bud Man an advertising/premium doll for Budweiser Beer, circa 1960s, $75.00. *Courtesy Cathie Clark.*

11½" vinyl Mattel Barbie Collector's Edition Little Debbie, U.S. Trademark of Mattel, Inc., except for Little Debbie which is a Trademark of McKee Baking Co., circa 1992, $50.00. *Courtesy Iva Mae Jones.*

Advertising Dolls

16" cloth Ronald McDonald doll, $35.00, and Big Mac vinyl hand puppet, $25.00, with McDonald village, $15.00, circa 1970s. *Courtesy Shirley Meade.*

9" hard plastic Fab/Luster Créme advertising walker doll with sleep eyes, mohair wig, original dress, circa 1958, $85.00. *Courtesy Jo Barckley.*

20" hard plastic Hasbro Ronald McDonald with cloth body, red cord around neck missing red plastic whistle which could be inserted in mouth to make noise when chest is squeezed, circa 1978, $25.00. *Courtesy Angie Gonzales.*

Buddy Lee

Buddy Lee is a display doll made for the H. L. Lee Company to promote Lee uniforms and was first offered to dealers in 1922. The Lee Company's most popular dolls were the Cowboy and Engineer reflecting their production of denim jeans and overalls. The early 12½" dolls were made in composition and the later 13" in hard plastic in about 1949. This is one doll that really appeals to men — especially men who wore uniforms in their work on the railroad, at gas stations, and Coca-Cola plants. It was discontinued in 1962. Collectors can look for outfits including Coca-Cola, Phillips 66, Sinclair, MM, Standard, John Deere, TWA, Cowboy, Engineer in striped and plain denim, and also two versions (farmers) dressed in plaid shirt and jeans.

13" composition cowboy advertised Lee Rider Overalls, circa 1920+, $350.00.
Courtesy Sherryl Shirran.

12" hard plastic, paper hatband on cowboy hat reads *Ride 'Em in Lee Rider Cowboy Pants,* in original red print shirt, red bandanna, jeans, circa 1950s, $400.00.
Courtesy McMasters Doll Auctions.

Advertising Dolls

12" composition, painted eyes to side, closed smiling mouth, molded and painted hair, composition body, jointed at shoulders, painted black boots, circa 1920+, $375.00. *Courtesy McMasters Doll Auctions.*

13" hard plastic Buddy Lee in tagged engineer overalls, missing cap, very good condition, circa 1950s, $375.00. *Courtesy June Algeier.*

13" hard plastic Buddy Lee gas station attendant, with MM labeled shirt and hat, possibly Minute Man service station, circa 1950s, $325.00. *Courtesy Louise Williams.*

The Gerber Baby

1936 – 1939

Gerber Products of Fremont, Michigan, first offered an all-cloth baby based on a drawing of Ann Turner (Cook) produced by an unknown manufacturer in 1936 through 1939. The premium doll was 8" tall and was available for 10 cents and three Gerber labels. It came in pink or blue silk-screened on cotton sateen. There followed six other licensed manufacturers who also produced premium dolls for the company.

1955 – 1959

From 1955 to 1959 Sun Rubber of Barberton, Ohio, produced an all-rubber 12" drink and wet baby sculpted by Bernard Lipfert. It was offered for $2.00 plus 12 labels or box tops. A Canadian version was made by Viceroy/Sunruco Company of Canada in 1955. The 12" Gerber Baby was also for sale retail and had variations in 13" and 18" sizes. It had a molded top knot, sleep eyes and was a drink/wet baby.

1965 – 1967

Arrow Rubber and Plastic Corp. produced a 14" doll dated 1965. She was sold as a premium for $2.00 and 12 Gerber labels or box tops.

1972 – 1973

Amsco Company produced 10" Gerber Babies in black and white with yellow molded hair instead of brown, a less noticeable top knot, and painted eyes instead of sleep eyes. The dolls molded hair varies with premium and retail models as does mouth size. They came with a variety of rompers, sleepers, and dresses. They added 14" and 18" sizes as well as accessories like a highchair and miniature Gerber Baby products, bowls, and spoons. They were marked "The Gerber Baby//Gerber Products Co.//19©72."

1979 – 1985

Atlanta Novelty Company was licensed to produce a 17" long 50th Anniversary doll, with soft cloth stuffed body, molded vinyl head, arms, and legs, "floating" flirty eyes, and open/closed mouth with molded tongue. It came in a blue, red, or yellow checked body suit trimmed white rickrack, a white eyelet bib, and an apron. They were marked on the back of the neck "Gerber Products Co.//© 1979." Dolls were issued in limited edition bisque. In 1981 a 12" doll, in 1982 a 12" doll, and in 1983 10" twins (who did not have flirty eyes) were produced. In 1985, both 12" and 17" dolls were produced in all-vinyl. All except the bisque came as black or white and all except the 1983 twins are marked with the Gerber name and year of manufacture.

There were variations in costumes with lace aprons and dresses and rompers, some dolls came with criers. A novel variant was a drink-and-wet doll with a cloth body. Another variant was the all-vinyl 12" Bathtub Baby available as a premium for $7.95 and three UPC symbols. A musical version with plush body was made in 1984.

1982 – 1992

Lucky Ltd. produced all-vinyl or vinyl with cloth body Gerber baby dolls in 6", 11", 14", and 16" sizes. They were marked on the back of the neck "©1989//Gerber Products Co." Some may have a Lucky Ltd. label in the side seam of their cloth body. The 6" size is jointed only at the neck and has the Lucky rabbit trademark on its back. The 11" size comes as a drink-and-wet baby with the rabbit trademark and had various costumes. The 14", 16", and 21" dolls have a cloth body with Lucky trademark and name on a seam label.

Advertising Dolls

1994 – 1996

Toy Biz, Inc. made all-vinyl 15" babies with painted eyes, marked on the back of the neck "©1994 Gerber Products Co.//Toy Biz, Inc." They also made 15" vinyl babies with cloth bodies. In 1994, they advertised a computer type English talking baby and a bilingual Spanish/English talking baby was available in 1995. In 1995, they also had a battery-operated baby with cloth body that cooed, cried, and giggled when touched or moved. Variations included a 13" baby with velour body, an 11" baby with music box, twins, and an Hispanic baby. Other dolls included an 8" fruit-scented baby, a battery-operated alphabet singing baby, and a baby care set with baby and bib, bonnet, blanket, food jar, bottle, spoon, food dish, and toy bear.

For more information on Gerber babies, see *A Collector's Guide to the Gerber Baby* by Joan Stryker Grubaugh ©1986.

18" rubber, by Sun Rubber Co. Gerber Baby, marked *Gerber Baby//©Gerber Products Co.//Mfg. By//The Sun Rubber Co.//Barberton, Ohio USA,* squeaker, sleep eyes, drinks and wets, painted molded hair, circa 1955 – 1958, $150.00.
Private collection.

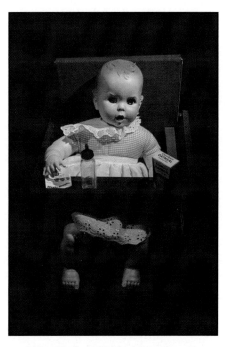

18" vinyl Atlanta Novelty Co. Gerber Baby, vinyl limbs with a blue and white checked cloth body, flirty eyes, painted molded hair, circa 1979, $50.00.
Courtesy Cathie Clark.

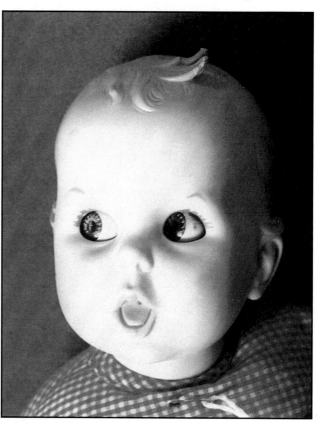

17" vinyl Atlanta Novelty Company Gerber Baby, with flirty eyes, vinyl limbs with red check stuffed cloth body suit, circa 1979 – 1985, $20.00.
Courtesy Espy Victoriano.

17" vinyl Atlanta Novelty Company 1979 Anniversary Gerber Baby with molded features, flirty eyes, blue checked cloth body suit, vinyl limbs, with rickrack on sleeves, white eyelet bib and apron, with wear, $20.00.
Courtesy Ruth Swalwell.

12" vinyl Atlanta Novelty Company Gerber Baby collector doll, open/closed mouth, flirty eyes, all original in white eyelet gown and basket, circa 1981, $100.00.
Private collection.

Alexander Doll Co.

The Alexander Doll Company made news on the financial pages as reorganization from their 1995 chapter 11 bankruptcy led new management to use the Japanese "kaizen" flow-type manufacturing. The company is owned by TBM Consulting Group and is located in the Harlem section of New York City. The new management has redesigned the production flow in the turn-of-the-century Studebaker plant to allow groups of workers to oversee the manufacturing process from start to finish on selected items. Instead of one person doing one job all day, the group works together to finish dolls within their group, thus increasing productivity and cutting costs.

The financial and production changes seem not to have slowed the interest in Alexander dolls which have increased in popularity under the guidance of the Alexander Doll collector's club, a company-sponsored marketing tool that also has been used successfully by both Effanbee during the 1930s and more recently by Vogue with their Ginny club.

Beatrice and Rose Alexander began the Alexander Doll Co. in about 1912. They were known for doll costumes, and began using the "Madame Alexander" trademark in 1928. Beatrice A. Behrman became a legend in the doll world with her long reign as the head of the Alexander Doll Company. Alexander made cloth, composition, and wooden dolls, and after World War II they made the transition to hard plastic and then into vinyl.

The doll world was shocked these past few years with skyrocketing prices paid for some wonderful collectible Alexander dolls at auction including $56,000.00 for an 8" hard plastic doll re-dressed as the Infante of Prague. Alexander's rare and beautiful dolls continue to attract young collectors. Alexander dolls continue to increase in value as shown by one-of-a-kind fully documented special dolls as they appear on the market. These should continue to gain in value with the support of the avid Alexander fans.

One of the Alexander company's luckiest breaks came when they obtained the exclusive license to produce the Dionne Quintuplets dolls in 1934. The Alexander Dionne Quintuples were introduced in 1935, and were made in both cloth and composition, as babies and as toddlers. Some of the rarer sets are those in the bathtub or with the wooden playground accessories like the carousel or Ferris wheel. Other companies tried to fill out their lines with matching sets of five identical dolls even though this brought copyright suits from Madame Alexander. Quintuplet collectors collect not only dolls, but clothing, photographs, and a large assortment of other related memorabilia.

Quint News is published quarterly at $10.00 per year by Jimmy and Fay Rodolfos, founders of a nonprofit group, Dionne Quint Collectors, PO Box 2527, Woburn MA 01888.

For photos of Alexander and other quintuplets see the Quintuplet section.

What to look for:

Alexander cloth dolls should be clean, all original, with bright colors. In newer Alexander dolls only mint, all original dolls with brochures, tags, boxes, and accessories bring top prices.

Composition Alexander dolls may have minute crazing, but must have good color, original clothes, labels, tags, and brochures to bring the highest prices. Buy dolls with severe cracking, peeling, or other damage *only* if they are all original or tagged.

Painted hard plastic are transitional dolls and may be mistaken for composition. Hard plastic dolls should have good color, tagged outfits, and be all original. The newer the doll, the closer to mint it should be. Alexander dolls were produced in the 1970s and 1980s with few changes — and collectors can find many of these dolls. The dolls from the 1950s and early 1960s are eagerly sought after as well as the limited edition special event dolls.

Composition

11" composition Butch, all original, blue sleep eyes, painted closed mouth, synthetic wig, cloth body, tagged romper suit outfit, circa 1942 – 1946, $200.00.

Courtesy Iva Mae Jones.

13" composition Alice in Wonderland, blue sleep eyes, with swivel waist, hang tag, original costume, circa 1930s, $525.00.

Courtesy McMasters Doll Auctions.

9" composition Dutch Boy, $155.00; and 9" composition Spanish Girl, $135.00; both all original with paper hang tags and labeled boxes, circa 1940s.
Courtesy McMasters Doll Auctions.

15" composition Jane Withers, brunette wig, tagged dress, cracks around eyes, fair condition, circa 1937 – 1939, $400.00.
Courtesy McMasters Doll Auctions.

17½" composition Madelaine, tagged coral dress, wrist tag, excellent condition, circa 1939 – 1941, $635.00; and 14" Bridesmaid, tagged yellow dress, wrist tag, near mint, circa late 1930s, $325.00.
Courtesy McMasters Doll Auctions.

13" composition McGuffey Ana, human hair wig, tagged dress, hang tag, circa 1937, $600.00.
Courtesy Betty Jane Fronefield.

15" composition Princess Elizabeth, sleep eyes, taffeta print dress, black velvet ribbon around waist, black velvet ribbon crown, rhinestone trim, circa 1937 – 1941, $550.00.
Courtesy Dee Cermak.

13" composition Princess Elizabeth, open mouth, tagged original dress, circa 1937, $525.00.
Courtesy June Algeier.

Alexander Doll Co.

19" composition Princess with marked wrist tag, tagged original dress, sleep eyes, open mouth, five-piece composition body, costume in unplayed-with condition, cracks near eyes and mouth, cloudy eyes, circa 1937 – 1941, $425.00. *Courtesy McMasters Doll Auctions.*

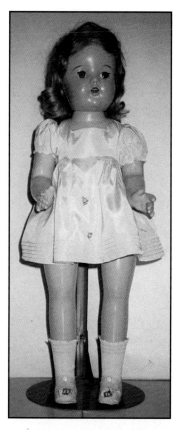

24" composition Princess Elizabeth, tagged Madame Alexander dress, blonde wig, cloth body, circa 1938 – 1939, $800.00. *Courtesy Dee Cermak.*

15" composition Princess Elizabeth re-dressed in copy of original outfit, circa 1937 – 1941, $300.00. *Courtesy Millie Busch.*

11" composition Scarlett
(Wendy Ann), tagged outfit,
excellent condition, circa 1937 –
1942, $600.00.
Courtesy Nancy Rich.

13" composition Snow White, original dress,
wrist tag, sleep eyes, light crazing, circa
1937, $400.00.
Courtesy Marie Emmerson.

Alexander Doll Co.

14" composition Sonja Henie, mohair wig, five-piece composition body in original tagged dress, including white skates, tag reads *Genuine "Sonja Henie" Madame Alexander N.Y. U.S.A.,* circa 1939 – 1942, $330.00.
Courtesy McMasters Doll Auctions.

18" composition Sonja Henie, excellent condition, original outfit, circa 1939, $995.00.
Courtesy June Algeier.

14" composition Sonja Henie, original dress, dimples in cheeks, mohair wig, eyeshadow over eyes, circa 1939 – 1942, $425.00.
Courtesy McMasters Doll Auctions.

Left: 13" composition Wendy Ann, brown sleep eyes, closed mouth, jointed waist, tagged pink dress, straw hat with flower trim, all original, circa 1935 – 1948, $190.00;
Right: 14" composition Madame Alexander Sonja Henie, brown sleep eyes, open mouth, four teeth, dimples, original human hair wig, jointed waist, original tagged skating outfit, replaced socks and skates, circa 1939 – 1942, $450.00.
Courtesy McMasters Doll Auctions.

13½" composition Wendy Ann, original costume lacks original hat and socks, circa 1935 – 1948, $300.00. *Courtesy Nancy Rich.*

Two 11" composition Little Pigs, marked *Madame Alexander, New York* on cloth tag, both wear original clothing, circa 1930s, $725.00.
Courtesy McMasters Doll Auctions.

Hard Plastic and Vinyl

18" hard plastic Binnie Walker, original outfit, Cissy face, circa 1954 – 1955, $400.00.
Courtesy Millie Carol.

15" vinyl Caroline in riding habit, all original, rooted hair, blue sleep eyes, open mouth, inspired by the daughter of John and Jackie Kennedy, produced in 1961 and 1962 only, $275.00.
Courtesy Iva Mae Jones.

9" hard plastic Cissette, boxed, original lace teddy, $210.00.
Courtesy McMasters Doll Auctions.

20" hard plastic Cissy, jointed
elbows and knees, high heel feet,
good color, Farm Girl outfit, shoes,
circa 1955 – 1959, $350.00.
Courtesy Darleen Foote.

20" hard plastic Cissy with original
tagged outfit, $300.00.
Courtesy McMasters Doll Auctions.

20" hard plastic Cissy Queen, jointed
elbows and knees, high-heeled feet, good
color, brocade costume, no earrings or box,
circa 1955, $600.00.
Courtesy Nancy Lazenby.

Alexander Doll Co.

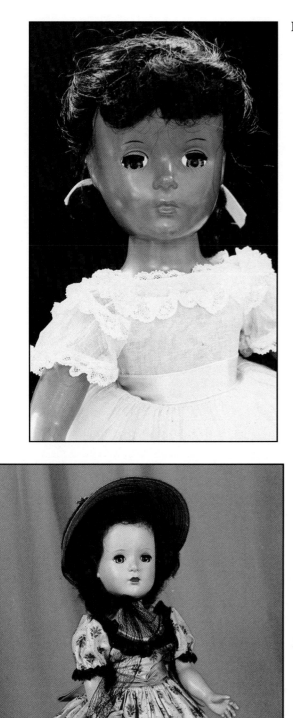

Rare black 15" hard plastic Cynthia, black wig, sleep eyes, all original tagged outfit, circa 1952, $795.00.
Courtesy Sally DeSmet.

8" vinyl Alexander-kin Dutch Boy, made first as a bent-knee walker or just with bent knees, 1961 – 1972, after 1973, dolls came with straight legs, in 1974 dolls were tagged Netherlands, $45.00+.
Courtesy Cathie Clark.

18" hard plastic Glamour Girl #2001C-Picnic Day, blue sleep eyes, closed mouth, synthetic wig, hard plastic body with walking mechanism, blue print gown, all original, circa 1953, $425.00.
Courtesy McMasters Doll Auctions.

21" vinyl Jacqueline in white
satin evening dress and matching coat, circa 1961 – 1962,
$850.00. *Courtesy Millie Busch.*

15" hard plastic Kelly in original
blue and white dress, replaced
shoes, no hat, circa 1959,
$275.00. *Courtesy Nancy Rich.*

21" hard plastic Margaret O'Brien,
original outfit, circa 1949 – 1951,
$1,125.00. *Courtesy June Algeier.*

31" hard plastic Mary Ellen walker, sleep eyes, closed mouth, saran wig, original costume, pale color, light wear on body, circa 1954, $215.00. *Courtesy McMasters Doll Auctions.*

30" hard plastic Mimi dressed in blue check original dress, made only for one year, multi-jointed body, pierced ears, sleep eyes, closed mouth, circa 1961, $450.00. *Courtesy Carol Bennett.*

10" hard plastic Southern Belle in her original white nylon dress with lace and green ribbon trim and a matching hat with red flowers, circa 1971 – 1973, $165.00. *Courtesy McMasters Doll Auctions.*

10" hard plastic Melinda Portrette in her picture box dressed in turquoise blue dress and white straw hat, tagged Melinda on dress, circa 1968 – 1969, $450.00.
Courtesy McMasters Doll Auctions.

10" hard plastic Scarlett in green taffeta dress trimmed in black braid, in original box, circa 1968, $425.00.
Courtesy McMasters Doll Auctions.

10" hard plastic Agatha Portrette, blue sleep eyes, synthetic wig, hard plastic jointed body, dressed in original red velvet dress with red velvet hat, original in her picture box, circa 1954, $215.00.
Courtesy McMasters Doll Auctions.

Alexander Doll Co.

10" hard plastic Renoir Portrette, mint in her original picture box, dressed in navy blue taffeta dress, black satin shoes, red taffeta hat, circa 1968, $350.00.
Courtesy McMasters Doll Auctions.

20" vinyl Pussy Cat, all original, brown sleep eyes, puckered mouth, cry/voice, cloth body, circa 1965, $100.00. *Courtesy Iva Mae Jones.*

8" hard plastic Quizkin Peter Pan, tagged inside vest, painted molded hair, sleep eyes, button on back moves head yes or no, circa 1953 – 1954, $500.00.
Courtesy Kim Vitale.

18" hard plastic Wendy Ann Bride in tagged costume, beautiful with original hair set, pretty color, circa 1948 – 1950s, $900.00.
Courtesy Cleveland Atkinson.

8" hard plastic Wendy and Billy in Harley Davidson motorcycle outfits, circa 1996+, $99.00 each, atop a new Buddy L motorcycle, $42.50.
Courtesy Nelda Shelton, Delightful Treasures.

Louis Amberg & Sons

Louis Amberg and Sons were in business from about 1878 until 1930. They were located in Cincinnati, Ohio, prior to 1898, and in New York City after that. They used other names before 1907. Amberg imported dolls made by other firms. They were one of the first manufacturers to produce all American-made dolls in quantities. As early as 1911, they made cold press composition dolls with straw-stuffed bodies and composition lower arms. In 1915 they introduced a character doll, Charlie Chaplin, which was a big hit for them. In 1918 Otto Denivelle joined the firm and introduced a hot press baking process for making composition dolls. Mibs, a soulful composition child with molded hair and painted eyes, was introduced in 1921. The company was soon making mama and Baby Peggy dolls. In 1927, they introduced the Vanta baby, which promoted Vanta baby clothing. In 1928 Amberg patented a waist joint and used several different heads on this torso, one of which was called the It doll. In 1930, Amberg was sold to Horsman who continued to make some of the more popular lines.

What to look for:

Amberg produced some very interesting composition characters, and being able to recognize these early dolls will be a plus for you. Labeled clothing, good color, and minimal crazing are points to keep in mind when searching flea markets, estate sales, or garage sales for these dolls.

13½" composition Edwina, marked *Amberg//pat. Pend.//LA&S C. 1928,* in old dress, painted molded hair, swivel waist, painted eyes, circa 1928, $375.00.
Courtesy Dorothy Bohlin.

American Character

American Character Doll Co. (1919+, New York City) first made composition dolls. In 1923 they began using Petite as a tradename for mama and character dolls. They later made cloth, hard plastic, and vinyl dolls. American Character Toni dolls from the late 1950s are an interesting reflection of society's acceptance of women and girls focusing on primping and beauty, concentrating on hair. The "Which twin has the Toni" ad campaigns and dolls used to advertise Toni Permanent Waves were common to the era. Toni, Sweet Sue, Tressy, Mary Makeup, and other dolls with high heels and fashion-type figures all reflect the focus on women as objects of beauty that remains an ongoing theme in dolls.

What to look for:

Composition American Character dolls should have good color, little crazing, and tagged original outfits or appropriate copies of original costumes using natural or period fabrics.

Hard plastic and vinyl dolls should have great color, be clean, and should be dressed in original costumes with tags, labels, and brochures intact. Again, the newer the doll, the more complete and closer to mint it must be to command higher prices. Reject soiled or nude dolls unless they have wonderful color and you have original clothes you can use to re-dress them.

Composition

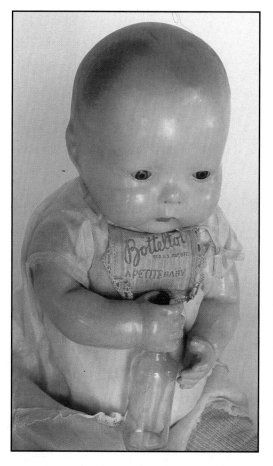

13" composition Botteltot, tin sleep eyes, closed mouth, painted hair, hand molded to hold bottle, cloth body, with original bib and dress, replaced bottle, circa 1926, $250.00. *Private collection.*

12" pair of composition Campbell Kids, painted side-glancing eyes, painted molded hair, excellent condition, original clothes, circa 1923, $1,200.00 for pair.
Private collection.

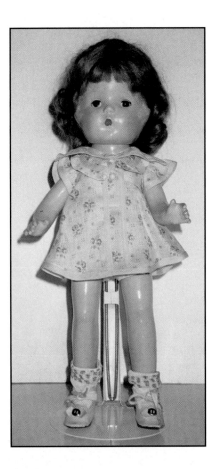

13½" composition Carol Ann Berry, marked *Petite,* brown sleep eyes, red mohair wig with small braid across top of head, all original Twosome costume, playsuit under dress of same material, circa 1935, $400.00.
Courtesy Dee Cermak.

20" composition Chuckles, original costume, lovely color, circa 1943, $250.00.
Courtesy Nancy Rich.

20" composition mama doll with tin eyes, mohair wig, cloth body with swing legs, crier, original clothes, circa 1920s, $350.00.
Courtesy Joanne Morgan.

24" composition Petite mama-doll, blue sleep eyes, open mouth, four teeth, mohair wig, cloth body, composition arms, lower legs, pink ruffled dress and bonnet, boxed, all original, circa 1923+, $475.00.
Courtesy McMasters Doll Auctions.

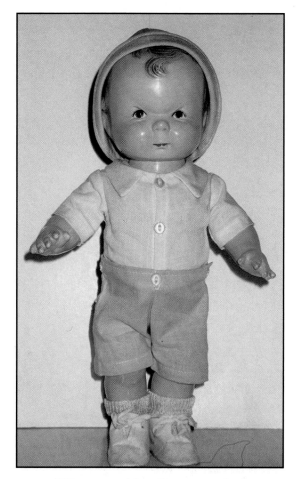

13" composition Puggy marked *A//Petite//Doll,* original outfit, circa 1928, $475.00. *Courtesy Dee Cermak.*

17" composition Petite Sally, a Patsy look-alike, original dress, circa 1930s, $275.00.
Courtesy Betty Jane Fronefield.

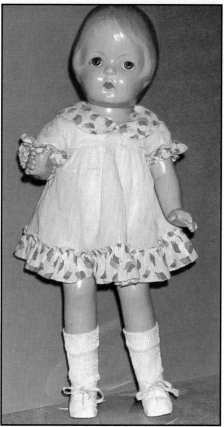

Hard Plastic and Vinyl

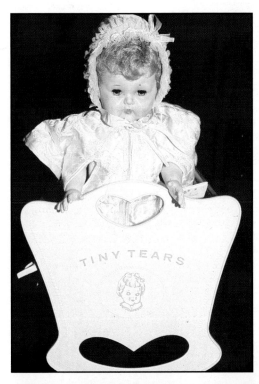

13" hard plastic Tiny Tears, vinyl body, synthetic wig, tiny tear holes next to the eyes, with her original cradle, circa 1952, $200.00. *Courtesy Cathie Clark.*

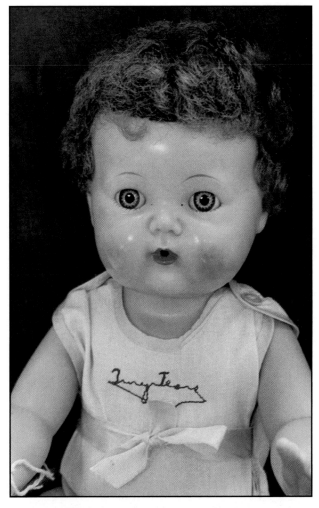

16" hard plastic Tiny Tears, a drink and wet doll, in original romper, vinyl body, circa 1950 – 1962, $125.00. *Courtesy Sharon Kolibaba.*

12" hard plastic Tiny Tears, rubber body, in layette box with accessories, circa 1950+, $350.00.
Courtesy Irene Grundtvig.

11" hard plastic Tiny Tears, vinyl body, sleep eyes, open mouth for bottle, all original with box and accessories, circa 1962, $425.00.
Courtesy McMasters Doll Auctions.

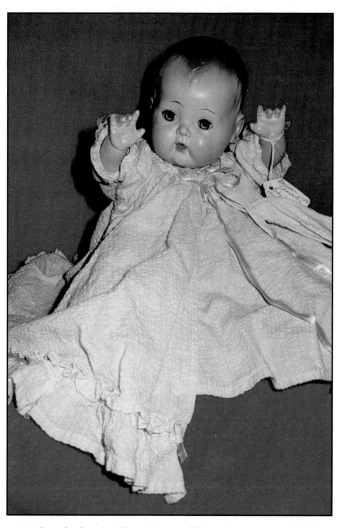

14" hard plastic Tiny Tears, blue sleep eyes, drink wet doll, rubber body, re-dressed, circa 1950s, $65.00. *Courtesy Millie Carol.*

10½" vinyl Toni Bride, mint in box, with brochures, circa 1950s, $200.00.
Courtesy Nancy Lazenby.

10½" vinyl Toni in marked original felt outfit, lovely color, sleep eyes, rooted hair, high
heel doll, circa 1958, $175.00.
Courtesy Kathy & Roy Smith.

10½" vinyl Toni, rigid vinyl body,
soft vinyl head with rooted hair,
sleep eyes, circa 1958, $125.00.
Courtesy Cathie Clark.

20" vinyl Toni, all original high
heeled doll with bag of accessories, circa 1958, $475.00.
Courtesy June Algeier.

29" vinyl Toodles, blue sleep eyes, open mouth/nurser, rooted saran hair, cry voice, fully jointed, re-dressed, rare size, circa 1960, $225.00.
Courtesy Iva Mae Jones.

20" vinyl Whimsie, original dress, rooted hair, painted eyes, freckles, watermelon mouth, synthetic hair mussed, great character face, circa 1960s, $75.00.
Courtesy Joanne Morgan.

21" vinyl Zack the Sack, one-piece stuffed body with molded head, painted molded eyes, closed smiling mouth, circa 1960, $40.00, and W.C. Fields, $800.00, probably by Effanbee.
Courtesy Cathie Clark.

Tressy

American Character introduced their Tressy in 1963, an era of high fashion where Jackie Kennedy increased interest in television, glamour, modeling, and fashion. Tressy's brochure described her as coming from a small town to the big city with a suitcase full of dreams to debut as Miss American Character, the most beautiful girl in the country. Tressy had a lot of fashions and accessories plus grow-hair operated by a button on her tummy with a key. The grow-hair was described as the *Secret Strand.* Tressy is 12" tall, with rooted grow hair in blonde, brunette, or red, heavy makeup, a rigid vinyl body and legs, and vinyl arms. She is jointed at neck, shoulders, hips, and has high-heeled feet. She is marked *American Doll & Toy Corp.//19©63* in a circle on her head. A competitor to Barbie, Tressy had extra accessories — hair glamour paks and separate costumes available.

Another variant, Mary Make-up was the same size as Tressy and came with make-up. Another part of this group was Cricket, Tressy's little sister.

11½" vinyl high heel V-leg Tressy, circa 1963, $100.00, has wide spaced legs that form a V when the doll is seated, with three new Tressy Magic Make-Up Face, circa 1965 – 1966, $80.00+ each. *Courtesy Debby L. Davis.*

Left: 11½" vinyl Mary Make Up on left, with beige eyeliner, not a grow-hair doll, straight legs, circa 1965 – 1966, $75.00; Right: Magic Make Up Face Tressy, blue eyeliner, grow hair feature, bendable legs, circa 1965 – 1966, $100.00. *Courtesy Debby L. Davis.*

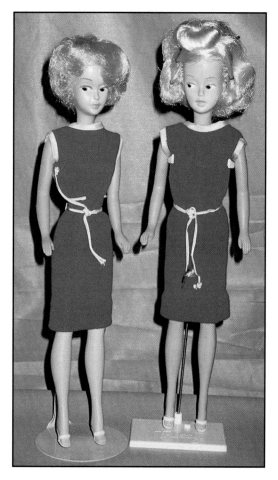

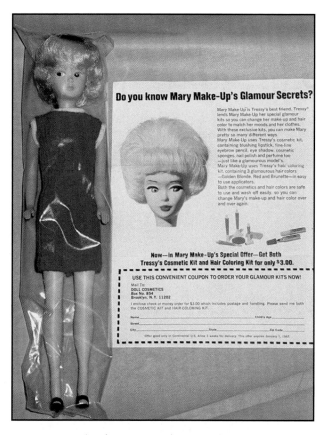

11½" vinyl Mary Make Up, described as Tressy's friend, shows off her original bubble cut platinum hairstyle, with hair glamour kits order form, $75.00, circa 1965. *Courtesy Debby L. Davis.*

11½" vinyl Tressy produced under license by Regal Toy Ltd. of Canada, with box labeled in French and English, and brochures, circa 1964 – 1966, $125.00. *Courtesy Debby L. Davis.*

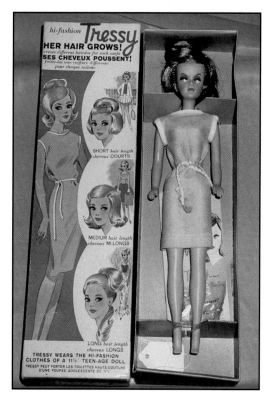

11½" vinyl Tressy gift set, 1963 –
1966, $200.00.
Courtesy Michael LaRusso and David Shall.

9" vinyl Cricket, the pre-teen sister of
Tressy, bendable legs, gift set, circa 1964 –
1966, $150.00.
Courtesy Michael LaRusso and David Shall.

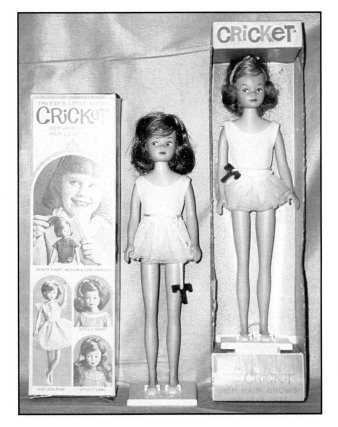

9" vinyl Cricket, the pre-teen sister of
Tressy, bendable legs, with box, marked
Amer Char//1964 on head, $75.00.
Courtesy Debby L. Davis.

14" vinyl pre-teen Tressy marked
Am. Char. 63 on head, made only
in 1963, $150.00.
Courtesy Debby L. Davis.

11½" Tressy under
license to Palitoy of
England, circa 1970,
$55.00; outfit is called
Motoring Miss $25.00.
Courtesy Debby L. Davis.

Arranbee

Arranbee Doll Co. was located in New York from 1922 until 1958. It was sold to Vogue Doll Co. who used the molds until 1961. Some of their bisque dolls were made by Armand Marseille and Simon & Halbig. They made composition baby, child, and mama dolls. Early dolls have an eight-sided tag. They went on to make hard plastic and vinyl dolls, many using the R & B trademark. Some hard plastic and vinyl dolls (Littlest Angel and Li'l Imp) were made for Vogue by the Arranbee division and may be marked by either.

What to look for:

Composition dolls should have good color, only very fine crazing if any, and original clothes or appropriate copies. Always look for mint-in-box and tagged dolls in excellent to mint condition. Hard plastic and vinyl dolls should be clean with bright rosy cheek color, tagged or labeled clothes, preferably with brochures and/or boxes to command higher prices in the future.

Composition

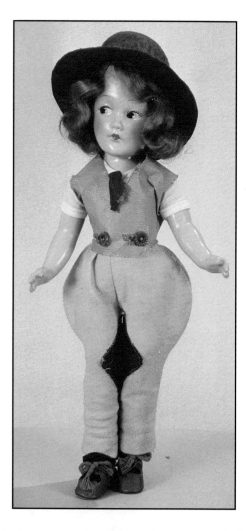

11" composition Debu' Teen in tan jodphurs with blue leatherette vest, white shirt, and brown felt hat, blue painted side-glancing eyes, mohair wig, circa 1939, **$375.00.** *Courtesy Peggy Millhouse.*

**14" composition Debu' Teen
in original ski outfit with
wooden skies and poles,
hang tag, circa 1940,
$475.00.**
Courtesy Peggy Millhouse.

17" composition Debu' Teen with original human hair wig, five-piece composition child body, original outfit with paper tag, general light crazing, circa 1940s, $225.00. *Courtesy McMasters Doll Auctions.*

13½" composition Kewty, side-glancing painted eyes, painted molded hair, bent arm, marked Kewty on back, re-dressed, circa 1930s, $225.00.
Courtesy Janet Hill.

14" composition marked Kewty, a Patsy-type, molded hair, side-glancing painted eyes, lovely color, circa 1930s, $275.00.
Courtesy Bev Mitchell.

19" composition Nancy, mint-in-box, paper tag, circa 1940, $600.00.
Courtesy Betty Jane Fronefield.

17" composition Nancy, circa 1930s, $325.00. *Courtesy Kay DeMattei.*

15" composition Nancy in original long dress, eyeshadow on blue tin eyes, mohair wig, circa 1939+, $275.00. *Courtesy Dee Cermak.*

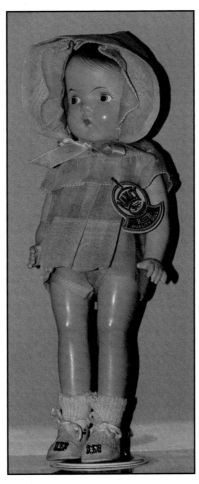

12" composition Nancy, original with tag, circa 1930s, $300.00. *Photo Bob Trowbridge, Mary Lu Trowbridge collection.*

14" composition Nancy Lee, all original in blue organdy, cotton slip, attached panties, with hang tag, sleep eyes, mohair wig, beautiful color, circa 1936 – 1938, $450.00.
Courtesy Peggy Millhouse.

14" composition Nancy Lee with mohair braids, eyeshadow over sleep eyes, red shirt, braided suspenders and trim around neck, replaced white hat, circa 1938 – 1941, $250.00. *Courtesy Peggy Millhouse.*

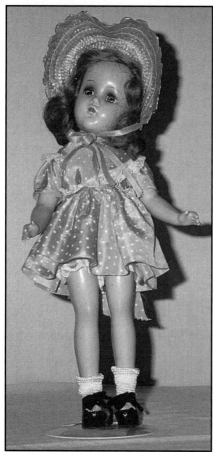

14" composition Nancy Lee, human hair wig, sleep eyes, original peach silk dress and hat, replaced shoes, circa 1939, $275.00.
Courtesy Gay Smedes.

9" composition Patsy-type girl, with painted molded hair, painted eyes, old yellow print dress, circa 1930s, $125.00.
Courtesy Janet Hill.

Hard Plastic and Vinyl

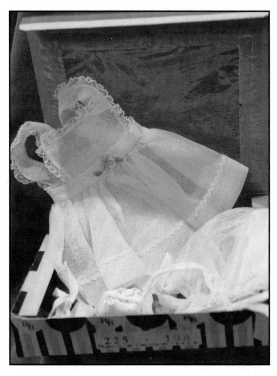

All-vinyl drink and wet Sweet Pea with rooted saran hair, mint in box with extra outfit, circa 1950s, $125.00. *Courtesy Pam Martinec.*

10" hard plastic Littlest Angel walker, rosy color, hair in original set, costume original except hat, has brochure, box, hang tag, circa 1956, $200.00.
Courtesy Gay Smedes.

10" hard plastic Littlest Angel walker in majorette costume, added feather, circa 1956, $175.00. *Courtesy Gay Smedes.*

14" hard plastic Nanette, original white nylon gown with peplum, picture hat, center snap leatherette shoes, circa early 1950s, $200.00.
Courtesy Mary Fudge.

Artist Dolls

These are original, one of a kind, limited edition, or limited production dolls of any medium (cloth, porcelain, wax, wood, vinyl, or other material) made for sale to the public. While a hot debate goes on in some doll-making and collecting circles as to the exact definition of an artist doll, we will use the above definition in this category. Some dolls appear to be works of art and some collectors may wish to have just that in their collection. Others define a doll as a play object and like to collect them for such. You, as a collector, are free to make your own decision to suit yourself. Still we can all appreciate the creativity which these talented artists exhibit.

What to look for:

One should remember that as with all collectibles, a well-made object of beauty will always be appealing. Some, not all, will increase in value. Study the dolls to find what you like. Some may only be popular fads.

A doll that is artistically done, in proper proportion stands a greater chance of increasing in value over time. You can enjoy it as part of your collection, rather than acquiring it entirely as an investment.

With artist dolls, one needs six examples or more of the artist's work to show the range of their talent. The artist doll category, however, does offer something for everyone.

Alphabetically by Maker

22" of Sculpey Pioneer Katie by Wendy Brent, Rose Petal Dolls, glass eyes, all original, circa 1979, $350.00.
Courtesy Betty L. Crosby.

**18" cloth character by Akira Blount,
NIADA artist, 1997, $395.00.**
Private collection.

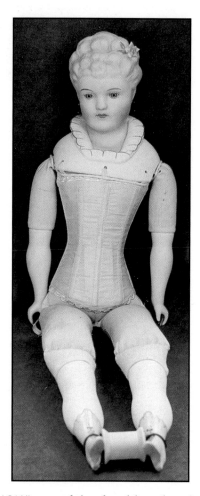

**18½" porcelain shoulder plate by
Emma Clear, painted molded hair,
floral decoration, painted eyes,
cloth body with porcelain limbs,
circa 1950s, $275.00.**
Courtesy Lisa Bolli.

**18" composition Dewees
Cochran Little Miss of 1936,
thread wig, cloth body, all
original, $2,000.00.**
Courtesy Millie Busch.

17" composition Dewees
Cochran Jennifer portrait doll,
tagged and signed, all original,
circa 1953, $2,000.00.
Courtesy Millie Busch.

13" porcelain Red Riding Hood by
Diana Effner, mint in box, hang tag,
circa 1988, $125.00. *Courtesy Millie Carol.*

21" vinyl limited edition doll by
Julie Good-Kruger, Circus Trainer,
all original with tags, 1990s,
$275.00. *Courtesy Millie Carol.*

21" porcelain Figure Eights by Julie Good-Kruger, limited edition of 1,000, holding 4½" stuffed penguin, tagged, all original, circa 1990s, $250.00. *Courtesy Millie Carol.*

18" vinyl by Julie Good-Kruger, circa 1989, $200.00. *Courtesy Millie Busch.*

26½" vinyl Annette Himstead Kai, all original, circa 1989, $900.00. *Courtesy Elizabeth Surber.*

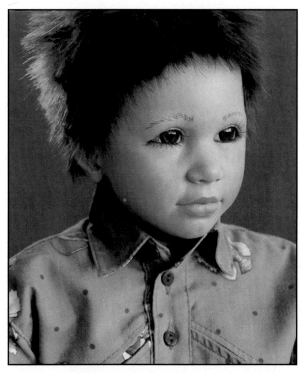

22" vinyl Annette Himstead Timi, one of the barefoot children, vinyl arms and legs, cloth body, original clothes, 1986+, $600.00. *Courtesy Millie Carol.*

32" vinyl Annette Himstedt
Ellen, circa 1985 – 1986,
$750.00. *Courtesy Cherie Gervais.*

29" vinyl Annette Himstead
Friederika, all original, circa 1988,
$2,200.00. *Courtesy Elizabeth Surber.*

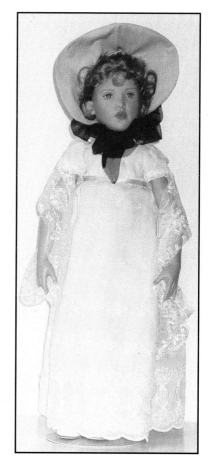

16" hard vinyl Viginia by
Helen Kish, circa 1997,
$250.00. *Courtesy Jill Sanders.*

21" vinyl Nettie Simplicity by Lee Middleton, with glass eyes, open/closed mouth with two molded teeth, dimples, synthetic wig, original wine corduroy outfit with black trim, circa 1978, $100.00. *Courtesy Helga Cunha.*

18" porcelain and cloth artist piece by Ann Mitrani, Fance, NIADA artist, 1997, $21,000.00. *Private collection.*

35" vinyl Bruno Rossellini Jackie Bouvier child, head and limbs made of hard-cast vinyl with special process that gives porcelain texture, hand-stitched dress, hand-knitted anklets, lambskin shoes, cloth body, circa 1997, $495.00. *Courtesy Iva Mae Jones.*

20½" porcelain shoulder head Henry VIII by Kathy Redmond, cloth body, elaborately dressed, $100.00.
Courtesy McMasters Doll Auctions.

15" wax doll by Lewis Sorenson, Marie Antoinette elaborate costume, painted features, beauty mark on cheek, circa 1980s, $800.00.
Courtesy Debbie Crume.

17" black porce-
lain Exie and
Ernie by Linda
Lee Sutton, all
original, limited
edition of 40,
circa 1989,
$695.00. *Courtesy
Jaci Jueden.*

21" porcelain Allex-
is by Linda Lee Sut-
ton Originals,
porcelain limbs,
issued in 1995,
limited edition of
ten, $595.00.
*Courtesy
Linda Lee Sutton.*

17" porcelain Linda Lee Sutton Originals
Bird Watcher Twins with nested birds in
bush, limited edition of 15, porcelain limbs,
circa 1998, $995.00. *Courtesy Linda Lee Sutton.*

17" porcelain Linda Lee Sutton Originals Little Golfer, limited edition of ten, golf club, ball, and green included, circa 1998, $575.00.
Courtesy Linda Lee Sutton.

22" porcelain Linda Lee Sutton Originals Cricket, limited edition of 15, circa 1998, $595.00. *Courtesy Linda Lee Sutton.*

15" porcelain Linda Lee Sutton Originals Hansel & Gretel, limited edition of ten sets, $995.00; Hansel & Gretel Chalet, $195.00; circa 1998.
Courtesy Linda Lee Sutton.

18" porcelain Linda Lee Sutton Originals KoKo and the bear Nod, limited edition of ten, $550.00; Igloo, Ice Stool and Fish Accessories, $195.00; circa 1998.
Courtesy Linda Lee Sutton.

30" porcelain lady and 20" child Ladies in White by Linda Lee Sutton Originals, limited edition of five sets includes antique china head doll, circa 1996, $3,250.00.
Courtesy Linda Lee Sutton.

16½" porcelain Linda Lee Sutton Originals Soda Pop with Love, sculpted from her daughter at 24 months, with all-porcelain articulated swivel chest body, limited edition of 20, circa 1996, $895.00.
Courtesy Linda Lee Sutton.

18" cloth original by Shelly
Thornton, NIADA artist,
circa 1990s, $2,400.00.
Private collection.

14" porcelain Phyllis Wright
limited edition Jennifer, with
human hair wig, painted eyes,
original, circa 1990s, #2, limited
edition of 100, $250.00.
Courtesy Barb Hilliker collection.

20" maple wood limited edition
by DOLFI of Italy, circa 1986,
$75.00. *Courtesy Laura Jennine Jacobs.*

Georgene Averill

Georgene Averill (ca 1915+, New York City) made composition and cloth dolls operating as Madame Georgene Dolls, Averill Mfg. Co., Georgene Novelties, and Madame Hendren. Her first line included dressed felt dolls. She also made Lyf-Lyk and the Wonder line, and patented the Mama doll in 1918. She designed dolls for Borgfeldt, including Bonnie Babe. Her Peaches was a Patsy-type doll. A very talented designer and maker, she made wonderful cloth and composition dolls. The family had ties to Arranbee, as some in-laws worked in production at that firm. Averill's line of whistling dolls with bellows in the cloth body was clever and made to portray different occupations or ethnic backgrounds.

What to look for:

Georgene made dolls of cloth, composition, or early plastic type materials. Georgene Averill was known for her felt costumes and composition mama dolls with swing legs and criers. Search for bright and clean cloth dolls and labeled or tagged costumes on composition dolls with rosy cheeks and little crazing.

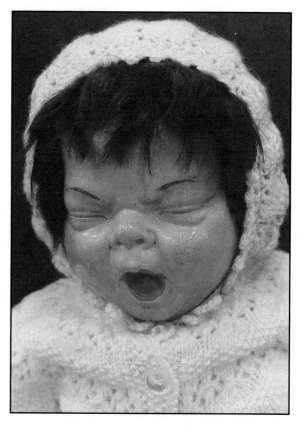

26" composition yawning baby, with asleep eyes, mohair wig, open/closed mouth, cloth body, marked *Georgene*, circa 1920s, $400.00. *Courtesy Teddy Callens.*

10½" composition Madame Hendren child in Dutch ethnic felt dress, painted side-glancing eyes, watermelon smile, mohair braids, circa 1930s, $165.00. *Courtesy Sharon Kolibaba.*

Georgene Averill

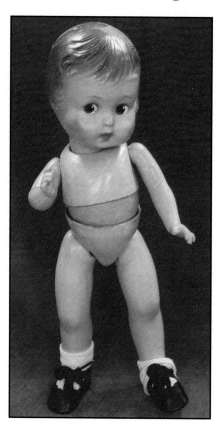

13½" composition Dimmie with jointed body-twist waist, ink stamp on body *Madam Hendron, Patent Pending,* circa 1929, $275.00.
Courtesy Bev Mitchell.

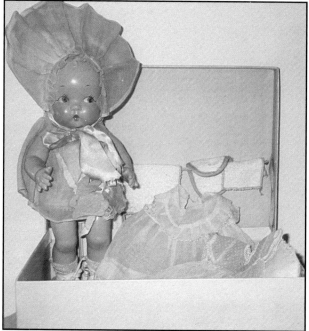

16" composition Little Cherub designed by and marked *Harriet C. Flanders,* in original box, hinged lid, two extra dresses, towel, two wash cloths, pillow, and socks, wears pink organdy dress and bonnet, circa 1937, $750.00.
Courtesy Dee Cermak.

Georgene Averill

14" composition Madame Hendren Little Sister designed by Grace Corey, molded blonde hair, old costume, circa 1920s, $395.00. *Courtesy Debbie Crume.*

20" composition Patsy-type girl with tin sleep eyes, open mouth with four upper teeth, white and orange tagged Madame Hendron dress, circa 1930s, $325.00. *Courtesy Bev Mitchell.*

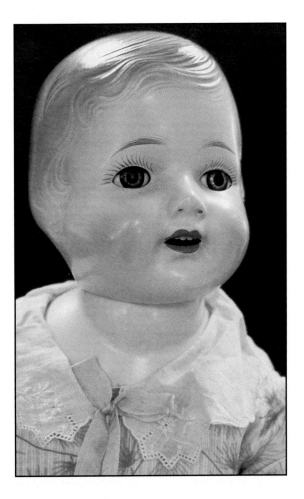

Barbie

Mattel began making Barbie doll in 1959 in Hawthorne, California. As we near the end of the century she remains a top collectible as children have grown up and become avid collectors of their childhood dolls. Of interest to collectors, also, are the fashion trends reflected by Barbie doll's seemingly endless wardrobe.

Marks:
1959 – 62: *BARBIE TM/PATS. PEND.// © MCMLVIII//by//Mattel, Inc.*
1963 – 68: *Midge TM © 1962//BARBIE ® / © 1958//BY//Mattel, Inc.*
1964 – 66: *© 1958//Mattel, Inc. //U.S. Patented//U.S. Pat. Pend.*
1966 – 69: *© 1966//Mattel, Inc.//U.S. Patented//U.S. Pat. Pend//Made in Japan*

Description of the first five Barbie dolls:
Number One Barbie, 1959
11½" solid heavy vinyl body, faded white skin color, white irises, pointed eyebrows, soft ponytail, brunette or blonde only, black and white striped bathing suit, holes with metal cylinders in balls of feet to fit round-pronged stand, gold hoop earrings.

Number Two Barbie doll, 1959 – 1960
11½" solid heavy vinyl body, faded white skin color, white irises, pointed eyebrows, no holes in feet, some with pearl earrings, soft ponytail, brunette or blonde only.

Number Three Barbie doll, 1960
11½" solid heavy vinyl body, some fading in skin color, blue irises, curved eyebrows, no holes in feet, soft ponytail, brunette or blonde only.

Number Four Barbie doll, 1960
11½", same as #3, but solid body of skin-toned vinyl, soft ponytail, brunette or blonde only.

Number Five Barbie doll, 1961
11½", vinyl head, now less heavy, hard plastic hollow body, firmer texture saran ponytail, and now also redhead, has arm tag.

What to look for:
Check those garage sales, flea markets, and estate sales for those first five Barbie dolls; even in played-with condition. Remember clean, undamaged, and original costumes should sound an alert. Barbie doll remains the number one collectible doll and has a huge following. Someone may be looking for those forgotten accessories and small items or body parts. It doesn't hurt to look in the attic at that old toy box, trunk, or carton that holds your forgotten toys from the sixties.

12" vinyl Harley Davidson Barbie, circa 1998, $250.00. *Courtesy Janet Santacruce.*

11½" vinyl Classique Series Benefit Ball designed by Carol Spencer, stock #1521, MIB, 1992, $200.00. *Courtesy Joann Colan.*

11½" vinyl Living Barbie, titian hair, pink lips, rooted eyelashes, bendable arms and legs, original outfit, near mint, circa 1970, $115.00.
Courtesy McMasters Doll Auctions.

Vinyl Living Skipper in box, #1117, circa 1970, near mint, $100.00; 11½" vinyl Living Barbie in box, #1116, near mint, circa 1970, $130.00.
Courtesy McMasters Doll Auctions.

6¼" vinyl Tutti in box, bendable/posable, circa 1966, $125.00; 6¼" Todd #3590, bendable/posable in box, circa 1967, $150.00; 9" Skipper, bendable legs, circa 1965, $300.00.
Courtesy McMasters Doll Auctions.

11½" vinyl Walk Lively Barbie in box, $175.00; Talking Busy Steffie in box, $315.00 and Talking Busy Ken, in box, $125.00, circa 1972.
Courtesy McMasters Doll Auctions.

11½" vinyl straight leg Midge, titian hair, pink lips, near mint, out of box, circa 1963, $140.00.
Courtesy McMasters Doll Auctions.

11½" vinyl Color Magic Barbie, lemon yellow hair, pink lips, original sunsuit, mint, circa 1966, $375.00.
Courtesy McMasters Doll Auctions.

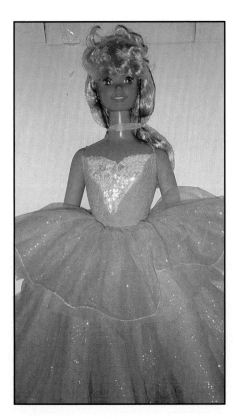

36" vinyl My Size Barbie, MIB, in glittery pink formal, circa 1993, $150.00.
Courtesy Iva Mae Jones.

**10" vinyl 35th Anniversary Barbie, mint
in box, circa 1994, $50.00.**
Courtesy Millie Carol.

**Barbie Transistor Radio, circa 1962,
$1,500.00.** *Courtesy McMasters Doll Auctions.*

Betsy McCall

Betsy McCall was a paper doll carried in *McCall's* magazine for many years. In about 1952 – 1953, Ideal had Bernard Lipfert design a doll based on that paper doll. This 14" Betsy McCall doll had a vinyl head, used a P marked Toni body, and had a glued-on saran wig. She was marked *McCall Corp.* on the head, and *Ideal Doll//P-90* on her back. She came with a McCall pattern for making an apron. In about 1958, American Character made an 8" hard plastic Betsy McCall, and in 1959, they made a 35" Betsy McCall with vinyl head and limbs and a plastic body. Today Robert Tonner has new releases of this childhood favorite.

What to look for:

Old *McCall's* magazines in the garage, attic, or basement with intact Betsy McCall paper dolls. Dolls should be clean with all body parts intact. These and the clothing to go with them can still be found. The large size can still be found in good condition.

Ideal

14" vinyl Ideal Betsy McCall with hard plastic body, original dress with attached petticoat, circa 1952 – 1953, $225.00.
Courtesy Mary Fudge.

14" vinyl Ideal Betsy McCall, hard plastic body, soft vinyl head, sleep eyes, glued on wig, uses the Toni body, circa 1952 – 1953, $150.00.
Courtesy Cathie Clark.

American Character

8" hard plastic American Character Betsy
McCall dolls, seven-piece body with jointed knees, original clothes, circa 1957+,
$85.00 each. *Courtesy Millie Carol.*

8" hard plastic American Character Betsy
McCall dolls with jointed knees, no
marks, circa 1957+, $150.00 each.
Courtesy Gay Smedes.

14" vinyl American Character Betsy
McCall with hard-to-find trunk and three
outfits, all original, circa 1961+, $525.00.
Courtesy June Algeier.

Black Dolls

A great collectible category is black dolls. Because fewer were made, black dolls almost always place over white dolls in competition. Fewer of these survived and finding one in mint condition is harder to do. These come in many different mediums and offer a wide range of collecting possibilities in cloth, composition, hard plastic, porcelain, rubber, and vinyl.

Shindana, 1968 – 1983, Los Angeles, California

After the Watts riots in Los Angeles, Shindana Toys was formed in 1968, the first major manufacturer of black dolls with ethnically correct features, high quality, covering a wide selection of babies, children, and adults. Shindana was a division of Bootstrap Inc., a non-profit black community organization founded by Lou Smith and Robert Hall. Its motto was "Learn Baby, Learn!" and they presented positive images of black children. It ceased production in 1983 and with a short 15-year span of operation, only a few of these dolls are still available. Dolls may be marked *Div. Of//Operation Bootstrap, Inc, USA//©1968 Shindana* or other Shindana marks.

What to look for:

Condition is still the number one factor in great collectible dolls. From finding a Leo Moss papier mache/composition to a modern vinyl, black dolls can be an intriguing part of your collection. Almost any out of production black doll mint in the box will remain a good collectible and may increase in value. Check for marks to find those Shindana dolls — they included the infamous O.J. Simpson as well as other celebrities. Do not overlook black dolls at garage sales and flea markets and other sales.

Cloth

13½" cloth baby with painted side-glancing eyes, yarn hair, oil cloth body, all original, circa 1940s, $195.00. *Courtesy Chantal Jeschien.*

Composition

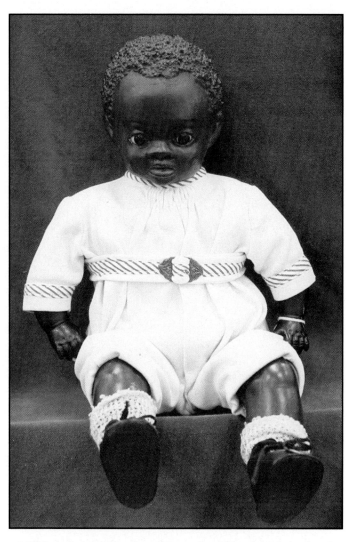

Rubber

16½" composition Leo Moss shoulder head, incised *LM//Dale* on back, dark cloth body, papier-mache arms and legs, glass eyes, heavily molded hair, pouty expression, circa 1880+, $3,700.00.
Courtesy O. Gregg.

20" rubber Effanbee Dy-Dee Baby, mint in box, #5700, applied ears, diaper, shirt, pacifier tied to wrist, distributed to American Red Cross, schools, and child care centers to teach pre-natal care, circa 1940+, $225.00.
Courtesy Iva Mae Jones.

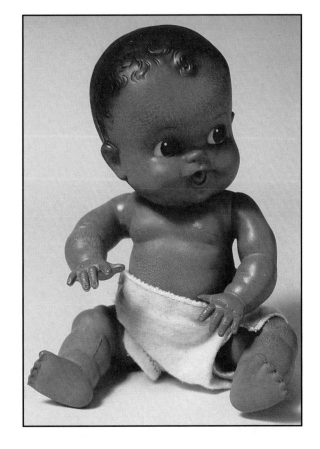

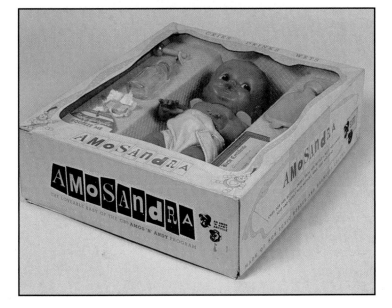

9½" all-rubber Amosandra designed by Ruth E. Newton, made by Sun Rubber Co. for EEGEE, circa 1940s, $175.00.
Courtesy Ursula Mertz.

Vinyl

13½" vinyl Shindana baby, rooted hair, ethnically correct features, drink and wet doll, first major manufacturer of dolls with correct ethnic features, circa 1972, $45.00.
Courtesy Marcie Montgomery.

20" all-vinyl child, marked *C. 1967//Beatrice Wright*, rooted hair, sleep eyes, re-dressed but has original outfit, circa 1967, $65.00.
Courtesy Marcie Montgomery.

13" vinyl Shindana baby, rooted hair, drink-and-wet doll, marked *Shindana, Div. Of//Operation Bootstrap Inc., USA//C. 1968*, $55.00.
Courtesy Marcie Montgomery.

23½" vinyl Gotz Yoramong by
Philip Heath, all original, circa
1990s, $600.00.
Courtesy Helga Cunha.

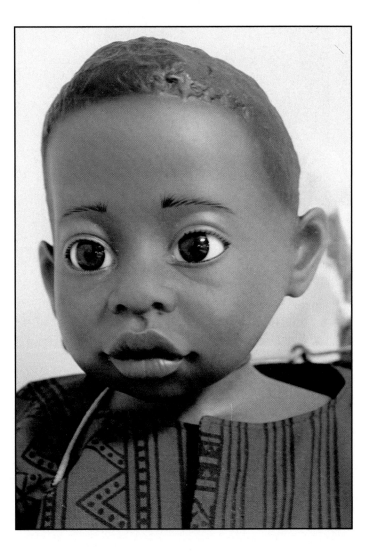

Cameo

Joseph L. Kallus's company operated from 1922 to 1930 in New York City and Port Allegheny, Pennsylvania. They made composition dolls with segmented wooden or cloth bodies, as well as all-composition dolls.

What to look for:

Look for dolls with good color, little or no crazing, and original costumes — especially those that bear labels. Look closely at the sewing on clothing; the inside part may reveal whether it was done by a home seamstress or was commercially made. Original clothing is always desirable; if it is intact you can use it on the doll — if not, you can use it for a pattern to re-create the style of costume your doll wore in the period she was made.

Avoid composition dolls with cracks, breaks, peeling, or lifting paint layers. Consider only if they have added attractions such as original clothing, labels, tags, boxes, or other accessories that may be salvaged for another doll.

Composition

10" composition Margie with wooden segmented body, molded hair, side-glancing painted eyes, circa 1929, $250.00. *Courtesy Odis Gregg.*

10" composition unmarked bow loop child, with wooden segmented body, molded shoes, similar to segmented dolls made by Cameo, circa 1930, $65.00. *Courtesy Bev Mitchell.*

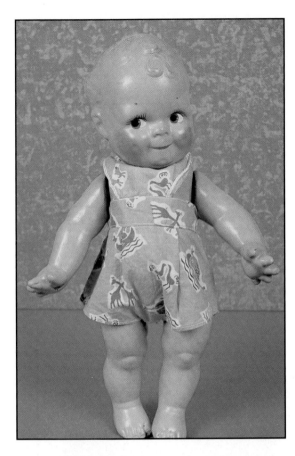

12" composition Scootles old print sunsuit, some paint rubs, flaking, circa 1925+, $250.00.
Courtesy McMasters Doll Auctions.

15" composition Scootles designed by Rose O'Neill, painted side-glancing eyes, paper hang tag, tagged original outfit, circa 1925+, $600.00.
Courtesy Jane Foster.

22" composition Scootles original red and white check romper, hard to find this large size, circa 1925+, $1,500.00. *Courtesy Janet Hill.*

Vinyl

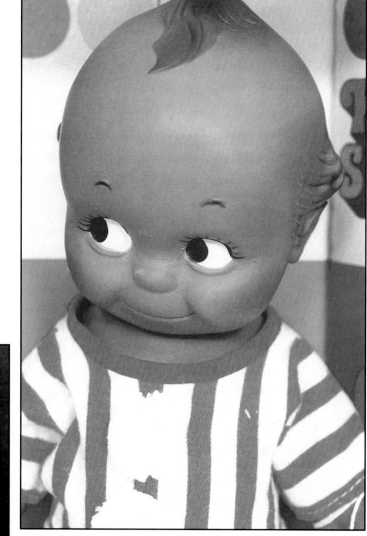

10" vinyl Kewpie, painted side-glancing eyes, watermelon mouth, hang tag, mint-in-box, circa 1984, $50.00. *Courtesy Carol Fairchild.*

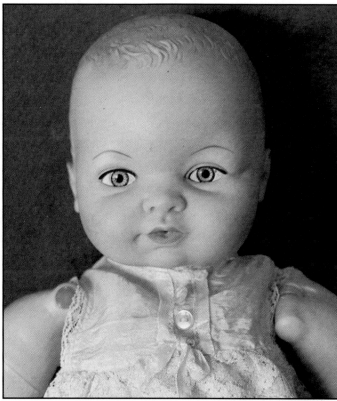

18" vinyl Miss Peep, pin-jointed arms and legs, played with, circa late 1960s, $45.00, if mint-in-box, $60.00. *Private collection.*

Celebrity Dolls

Celebrity dolls must represent real people — they cannot be a literary, comic, or cartoon character. They must represent someone who lived. To still be considered a celebrity doll, the doll may represent the person who plays the character on television, in the movies, or in a play. Abraham Lincoln was a real person so the Lincoln doll can be entered in the celebrity doll category. Princess Diana was a real person, so again, the doll that represents her can be considered a celebrity doll.

Charlie McCarthy was never alive — he represents an object and although he is famous as a ventriloquist's dummy from the movies, he is not a celebrity doll and would be disqualified in competition if placed in that category. Dorothy of Oz fame is not a celebrity doll — but Judy Garland, who portrayed the Dorothy character in the Wizard of Oz film, is regarded as a celebrity doll. Mickey Mouse is not a live person, he is a Disney cartoon or comic character and is not considered a celebrity doll.

This is an exciting, fun, very interesting category of collecting. While Shirley Temple is a celebrity, she is so collectible and so famous, the doll usually has its own category. The same is true for the Dionne Quints. Avid Quint and Shirley fans usually collect all sorts of accessories, ephemera, and related memorabilia as well as the dolls. You can collect just television or movie celebrities, athletes, black dolls, or whoever catches your fancy.

What to look for:

Condition and originality highly influence the collecting status of these dolls as well as associated boxes, labels, brochures, and other paper products. Look for clean dolls with original tagged or labeled costumes, good color, and related items that enhance the collector's knowledge of the doll.

Alphabetically by Celebrity

16½" vinyl Effanbee Lucille Ball, seventh in Legend Series, all original, circa 1985, $150.00. *Courtesy Debbie Crume.*

8½" vinyl Hasbro Charlie's Angels Kate Jackson as Sabrina, mint-in-package, circa 1977, $30.00. *Courtesy Irma Cook.*

8½" vinyl Hasbro Charlie's Angels Jaclyn Smith as Kelly, mint-in-package, circa 1977, $30.00. *Courtesy Irma Cook.*

8½" vinyl Hasbro Charlie's Angels Cheryl Ladd as Kris, mint-in-package, circa 1977, $30.00. *Courtesy Irma Cook.*

12½" Gilbert Sean Connery as James Bond, soft vinyl head, painted features, hard plastic body and vinyl limbs, body is marked Ideal since the body was made for the Tammy Family Ted doll, circa 1965, $50.00.
Courtesy Cathie Clark.

18" vinyl Dakin James Dean Special Edition, mint with box, circa 1985, $150.00.
Courtesy Debbie Crume.

11½" vinyl fully jointed Goldberger Prince Charles and Diana, Princess of Wales, painted eyes, MIB, circa 1982, $125.00 pair. *Private collection.*

19" Danbury Mint 1982 Diana, Princess of Wales, bridal dress, porcelain, $500.00. *Courtesy Kathryn Wolbers.*

20" Libby Barbara Eden as Jeannie from I Dream of Jeannie, all-vinyl, fully jointed, rooted blonde hair, blue sleep eyes with heavy painted lashes, marked © *1966//Libby,* circa 1966, $50.00. *Courtesy Cathie Clark.*

15" Ideal composition Judy Garland in Dorothy costume, with plush Cowardly Lion, $2,800.00. *Courtesy McMasters Doll Auction.*

15½" vinyl Shindana #1048
Marla Gibbs celebrity doll
from The Jeffersons TV
show, dressed in original
outfit, circa 1978, $45.00.
Private collection.

21" vinyl Baby Barry Toy Emmett Kelly as
Willie, the Clown, circa 1959, $290.00.
Courtesy Jeanie Hogh.

Mattel vinyl characters from the TV sitcom, Welcome Back Kotter, includes 9¼"
Gabe Kotter, played by Gabe Kaplan, and
9" John Travolta as Vinnie Barbarino,
circa 1976, set of five characters with
schoolhouse case, $215.00.
Courtesy Olivina Mata.

13" porcelain Historical Society President Abraham Lincoln and 11" wife, Mary Todd Lincoln, mint-in-box, limited edition of 2,500 with certificates, much historical detail, circa 1984, $1,800.00 for pair. *Courtesy Kathy & Roy Smith.*

11½" Eegee Dolly Parton and six outfits, all-vinyl
and fully jointed, rooted light blonde hair, painted
dark blue eyes and very pale complexion, circa
1978, doll $25.00, clothes $15.00 each.
Courtesy Cathie Clark.

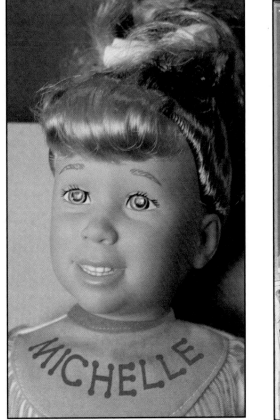

15" vinyl Michelle star of TV sitcom, Full
House, as portrayed by the Olson twins,
talker, mint-in-box, circa 1990, $45.00.
Courtesy Pauline Lyon.

18" vinyl World Doll Inc. Marilyn Monroe, mint-in-box, circa 1983, $200.00.
Courtesy Pauline Lyon.

13" all-cloth Richard Nixon, $75.00; 12" porcelain Franklin D. Roosevelt with cloth body, $75.00; both wearing campaign buttons, circa 1970s.
Courtesy Millie Busch.

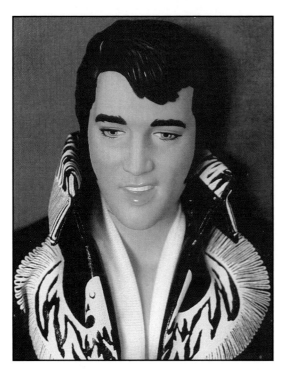

18" vinyl World Doll Inc. Elvis Presley in black jumpsuit, mint with box, circa 1984, $150.00. *Courtesy Pauline Lyon.*

20" porcelain Danbury Mint Nancy Reagan in inaugural gown, mint-in-box, circa 1980s, $200.00.
Courtesy Sandra Burklen.

23" porcelain Eleanor Roosevelt by doll artist Maggie Head, painted features, cloth body, circa 1940s, $200.00. *Courtesy Millie Busch.*

18" porcelain artist doll by Lita Wilson, NIADA, Elizabeth Taylor as Cleopatra, circa 1970s, $100.00. *Courtesy Millie Busch.*

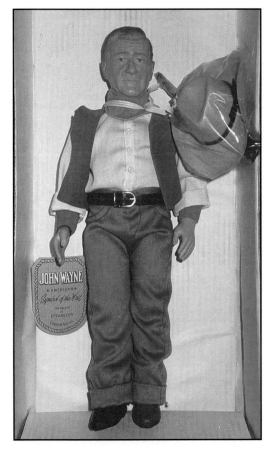

16" vinyl Effanbee John Wayne, mint-in-box, circa 1981, $95.00.
Courtesy Millie Carol.

Cloth Dolls

Cloth dolls have gained immensely in popularity with collectors recently. Because the doll is made of cloth, children have always favored them for their soft cuddly appearance. This category again presents a wide variety for the collector and while prices have skyrocketed in the past 10 years, there are still good buys to be found in some of the lesser known dolls that collectors have overlooked in their pursuit of more well-known examples.

What to look for:

Clean dolls with high color on the cheeks, not soiled, ripped, or torn, with original labels, tags, brochures, or boxes. A worn dirty doll will retain little value, so the buyer should consider again that main factor, condition, before purchasing. Do not pay huge prices for dolls that have rips, soil, fading, or other flaws – even if you do love it.

Alphabetically by Manufacturer

19" cloth girl with original dress, bonnet, yarn hair, mask face, plastic eyes, original teddy bear hang tag reads *AT Playtoys//Atlanta Georgia,* circa 1960s, $55.00. *Courtesy Debbie Crume.*

Cloth Dolls

2½" to 4½" cloth German Baps
fairy tale characters, $25.00 to
$60.00 per set. *Courtesy Sue Kinkade.*

4" cloth Baps Hans Brinker with 6" Mother, painted features, floss hair, metal feet, $65.00 for pair. *Courtesy Sue Kinkade.*

4" cloth Baps Mary, Quite Contrary made
in Germany, painted features, floss hair,
metal feet, $55.00. *Courtesy Sue Kinkade.*

13" cloth Chad Valley child, glass eyes, hang tag, original outfit, circa 1920s – 1930s, very good condition, $550.00. *Courtesy Sharon Kolibaba.*

20½" cloth Martha Chase boy, painted hair, features, cloth body and painted limbs, jointed elbows and knees, nicely dressed, some paint rubs, circa 1900 – 1920, $1,800.00. *Courtesy Elizabeth Surber.*

17" cloth boy, 16" girl, and 12" baby (not shown), Dollywood Defense Dolls, as shown in November 1995 Doll Reader, circa 1940s, $350.00 for set. *Courtesy Debbie Crume.*

12" cloth ethnic girl, painted features, side-glancing eyes, mohair wig, faded costume, circa 1950s, $42.00. *Courtesy Olivina Mata.*

17" cloth girl designed by Maud Tousey Fangel, printed features on stuffed cloth body, original outfit, some soil, circa 1930s, $475.00. *Courtesy Sharon Kolibaba.*

18" oil-painted cloth swivel head Kamkins with molded features, cloth body, old outfit, light wear, circa 1919 – 1928, $625.00. *Courtesy McMasters Doll Auctions.*

11" cloth child , Merrythought, England, with large glass eyes, mask face, with velvet and fur clothes made as part of body, tag left foot *Merrythought/Hygenic Toys/made in England/Regd. Design #809372,* circa 1930s, $425.00. *Courtesy Sherryl Shirran.*

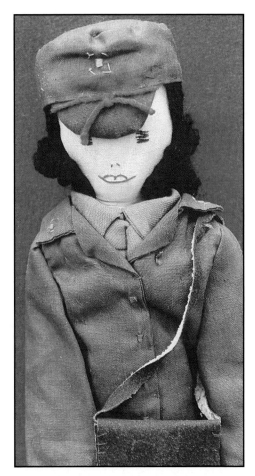

12" cloth handmade Molly, the Marine has paper pinned to dress, circa 1940s, $115.00. *Courtesy Marcie Montgomery.*

18" cloth Mollye's felt dressed Indian, mask face, nose rub, side-glancing eyes, circa 1920s+, $75.00. *Courtesy Debbie Crume.*

14" all-cloth Mollye's ethnic child with painted features, side-glancing eyes, bright regional clothing, made from the 1920s through the 1950s, $130.00.
Courtesy Nancy Rich.

11½" all-cloth Madam Hendron, a Mollye costume design, Dutch pair with painted features, side-glancing eyes, bright regional clothing, made from the 1920s through the 1950s, $95.00 each. *Courtesy Nancy Rich.*

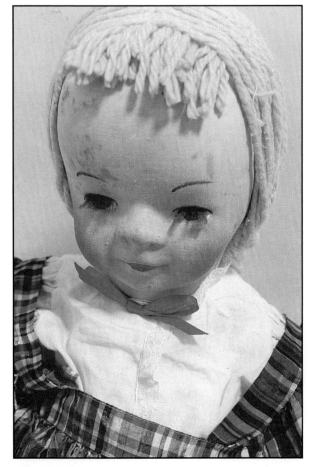

27" cloth Georgene Averill doll by Mollye with painted features, "real" eyelashes, yarn hair, original clothes, some stains, circa 1930s, $125.00.
Courtesy Chantal Jeschien.

18" cloth child designed by Eugenie Poir with mask face, painted features, mohair wig, wears copy of original outfit, has original underwear, shoes, and socks, circa 1930s, $500.00+.
Courtesy Millie Busch.

Pair of 17" cloth Eugenie Poir girls
with mohair wigs in marcelled style,
painted side-glancing eyes, original
clothing, circa 1920s, $700.00 each.
Courtesy Barbara DeFeo.

22" cloth unmarked child, possibly Raynal, painted side-glancing eyes, wig, felt clothes, circa
1930s, $300.00. *Courtesy Faye Newberry Gallagher.*

12" book marks with painted ¾" tall silk
faces, seam binding body with tiny leather
legs attached, felt hats add height, ruffled
ribbon collars, floss hair, labeled *Made in
France* circa 1920s, $50.00 – $75.00 each.
Courtesy Arthur Mock.

Comic

Comic characters are great collectibles and this category presents huge potential for the collector who is looking for something away from the mainstream. Not only characters from the comic pages of the newspapers, but comic books, movies, and television cartoon characters are included. These may come in many different mediums and the collector may wish to include associated paper goods or other accessories with the dolls.

What to look for:

Again condition is king when choosing collectibles. Dolls should be clean, with good color, little crazing if composition, and preferably with tags, boxes, labels, original clothing, all intact. Have fun looking for these dolls at garage and estate sales, on ebay, or in thrift shops — comic characters are a great collectible that men seem to like.

14" Georgene Novelties cloth Becassine, a cartoon character from a French publication *La Semaine de Suzette,* **with box, tags, circa 1953, $400.00+.** *Courtesy Sherryl Shirran.*

Left: 14" vinyl Ideal Joan Palooka, blue sleep eyes, circa 1953;
Right: Bonny Braids painted eyes, circa 1951 – 1953; painted molded hair, rooted tufts, stuffed rubber Magic Skin bodies, boxed, $775.00 for both.
Courtesy McMasters Doll Auctions.

Left: 18½" cloth Modern Toy Co. Buttercup, $150.00; Right: 15" Buttercup, $295.00; wire forehead curls, clothes all original, head marked *Buttercup/by permission of/Jimmy Murphy/copyright 1924 by/King Features Syndicate, Inc.,* from the cartoon strip "Toots & Casper," circa 1925. *Courtesy Sherryl Shirran.*

Set of four resin comic strip characters, Dagwood, Blondie, 5"; Alexander 4"; and Cookie 3"; marked *©. 1944 KFS, for King Fisher Syndicate,* painted molded one-piece figures, circa 1950s, $350.00 for set. *Courtesy Dolores Ortega.*

14½" composition Knickerbocker Dagwood comic strip character, original outfit, missing hat, circa 1930s, $650.00. *Courtesy Sherryl Shirran.*

10" composition Knickerbocker Alexander comic strip character, all original, circa 1930s, $375.00.
Courtesy Sherryl Shirran.

21" cloth Al Capp's Daisy Mae by Hol-Le Toy Co., NY, mask face, painted features, cloth body, molded bosom, mitt hands, bare feet, original outfit, excellent condition, $130.00.
Courtesy McMasters Doll Auctions.

14½" vinyl Dennis the Menace a comic strip character created by Hank Ketcham, molded yellow hair, freckles, brown eyes, open/closed mouth, circa 1955 – 1958, $25.00.
Courtesy Kathy & Roy Smith.

12" cloth Alvin, $2,000.00; 14" cloth Tubby Tom, $2,000.00; and 14" all-cloth Little Lulu by Marge, $1,300.00.
Courtesy McMasters Doll Auctions.

14" cloth Georgene Averill Little Lulu, swivel head, mask face, cloth body, original costume, red plastic purse, excellent condition, circa 1944+, $500.00.
Courtesy McMasters Doll Auctions

14" cloth Georgene Novelties comic character, Little Lulu mask face, painted features, some wear, circa 1944 – 1951, $375.00.
Courtesy Nelda Shelton.

14" cloth Georgene Novelties comic character Tubby Tom, mint-in-box, with paper hang tag, circa 1951, $1,000.00+. *Courtesy Elizabeth Surber.*

14" vinyl UPA Pictures Inc. Mr. Magoo comic character, all original, cloth body, circa 1962, $45.00. *Courtesy Kathy & Roy Smith.*

Left: 13½" cloth Georgene Novelties Sluggo, mask face, painted black eyes, closed smiling mouth, applied ears, cloth body jointed at shoulders and hips, all original, circa 1944 – 1951, $775.00; Right, 13" cloth Georgene Novelties Nancy mask face, large painted black eyes, closed smiling mouth, original black fuzzy hair, cloth body jointed at shoulders and hips, all original, circa 1944 – 1951, $850.00. *Courtesy McMasters Doll Auctions.*

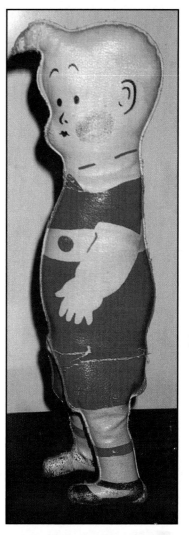

14" oilcloth pillow doll, Skeezix from the comic strip Gasoline Alley, circa 1920s, $225.00. *Courtesy Stephanie Prince.*

20" cloth Georgene Novelties literary character, Nurse Jane from the Uncle Wiggley series, all original, circa 1950s, $600.00. *Courtesy Debbie Crume.*

Composition Dolls

Composition dolls have been made since the 1890s and possibly earlier. Cold press composition describes the method of putting a mixture of ingredients (composition) into molds. The recipe for composition varied with each manufacturer, but at first glue was used to bind together such things as flour, shredded cardboard or paper, and rags. Later recipes used wood pulp as manufacturers learned how to bake the composition in multiple molds in the hot press method. The mixture was more soupy when poured into molds than when pressed and the ingredients differed somewhat.

These doll heads were first described as indestructible as compared to the bisque and china heads that could be easily broken. The dolls were dipped in tinted glue baths to give a flesh tone and then later the features and coloring were air-brushed. Humidity made it difficult for the dolls to dry correctly in early production procedures, but later techniques were refined to reduce this problem. The big problem with composition dolls was their glycerin and glue base — when the surface became saturated with water, it would disintegrate. Extremes in heat and humidity cause bacteria to grow on the surface and destroy the painted finish.

Collectors need to keep composition dolls away from direct sunlight, avoid extremes in temperature, and keep a gauge in their cases to check the relative humidity. When the relative humidity exceeds 85%, bacteria have opportune conditions to grow and destroy the painted surfaces. Composition dolls should not be stored in plastic, but wrapped in cotton fabric that has been washed and well rinsed to remove any soap or conditioner. Collectors who had this type of doll as a plaything in their childhood can, with a little caution, enjoy some of the wide variety of dolls still available. Included in this category are composition dolls by unknown makers or little known companies.

What to look for:

Great composition dolls should have no crazing, cracking, peeling, or lifting of paint. They should also have rosy cheek color and original wig and clothes. They may have blush on knees, hands, and arms. Added incentives would be tags, labels, brochures, or labeled boxes. Consider dolls with major flaws only if they have pluses like tagged original costumes, brochures, hang tags, or boxes, and they should be priced accordingly.

Baby or Toddler

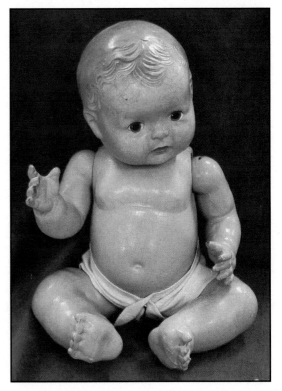

15" composition baby by unknown maker, unmarked, painted eyes, painted molded hair, jointed bent-leg composition body, came dressed in diaper, circa 1930, $150.00. *Courtesy Jean Thompson.*

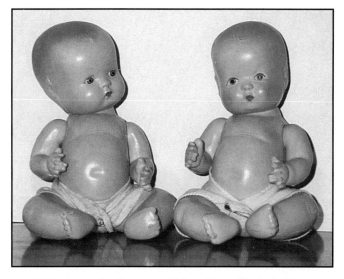

10" unmarked composition bent-limb babies, sleep eyes (left), painted eyes (right), with original diapers, circa 1930s, $100.00 each. *Courtesy Gay Smedes.*

15" composition baby, Dimples type, unmarked, bent-leg composition baby body, family doll, received Christmas 1932, $150.00. *Courtesy Susan Martin Olivo.*

7" composition bent-limb baby, painted blue eyes, molded and painted hair, original outfit, unplayed with condition, label on printed box reads *The Brownie House//Lucille Pierson//Laconia, NH* circa 1930s, $150.00. *Courtesy Gay Smedes.*

14" all-composition unmarked toddler, sleep eyes, painted molded hair, printed silk outfit, unplayed with condition, circa 1930s, $225.00. *Courtesy Gay Smedes.*

Composition Dolls

12" all-composition unmarked toddler, blue sleep eyes, brown molded and painted hair, original outfit, circa 1940s, $250.00. *Courtesy Dee Cermak.*

Child

15" unmarked composition girl, sleep eyes, mohair wig, original dress, attached undies, circa late 1930s, $200.00. *Courtesy Gay Smedes.*

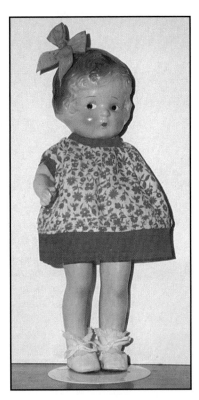

14" unmarked composition girl with molded loop for hair ribbon, painted side-glancing eyes, circa 1930s, $200.00. *Courtesy Gay Smedes.*

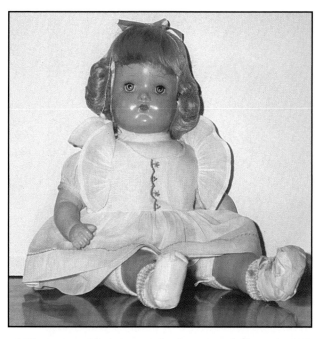

15" composition unmarked mama doll type with cloth body and crier, swing composition legs, blue tin eyes, mohair wig, original outfit, circa 1930s, $200.00. *Courtesy Gay Smedes.*

8" composition unmarked girl, painted side-glancing eyes, brown mohair wig, all original in blue velvet beret and jacket, wool plaid skirt, painted molded socks and shoes, circa 1930s, $175.00. *Courtesy Gay Smedes.*

22" composition unmarked mama doll, blonde mohair wig in original set, sleep eyes, cloth body with crier, original outfit, unplayed with condition, circa 1940s, $350.00. *Courtesy Gay Smedes.*

21" composition Gold Seal mama doll with flange head, sleep eyes, open mouth with two upper teeth, painted molded hair, cloth body with crier, composition arms and legs, original outfit, labeled box, circa 1930s, $150.00. *Courtesy McMasters Doll Auctions.*

12" composition Regal Bobbie Anne, a
Kiddie Pal Dolly, in suitcase trunk with
four extra original outfits, hang tag,
painted eyes, molded hair, bent arms,
circa 1930s, $400.00+.
Courtesy Elizabeth Surber.

12½" composition Maxine Mitzi, a
Patsy-type with painted eyes, bent
arm, original clothing, left foot touch-
up, circa 1929, $365.00.
Courtesy Debbie Crume.

11½" composition Fruendlich Trixbe,
all original with marked box, circa
1930s, $150.00. *Photo Bob Trowbridge,
Mary Lu Trowbridge collection.*

13" composition unmarked child with original thin muslin dress, painted eyes, molded hair, circa 1930s, $100.00. *Courtesy Bev Mitchell.*

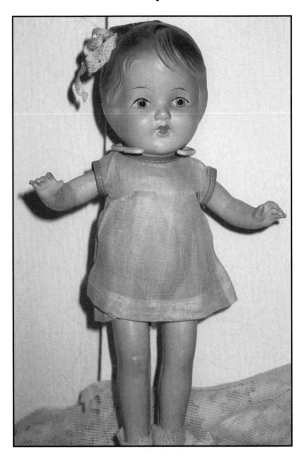

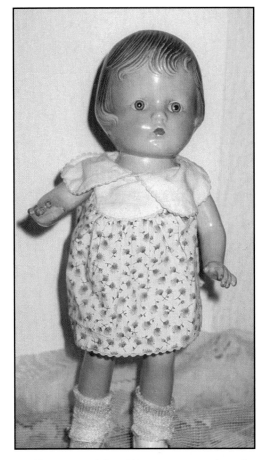

14" composition Patsy-type, painted molded hair, sleep eyes, bent right arm, lovely color, re-dressed, circa 1930s, $125.00. *Courtesy Bev Mitchell.*

18" composition Patsy-type with tin eyes, painted molded hair, both arms slightly bent, original dress, circa 1930s, $225.00. *Courtesy Bev Mitchell.*

Composition Dolls

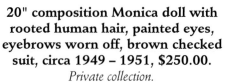

20" composition Monica doll with rooted human hair, painted eyes, eyebrows worn off, brown checked suit, circa 1949 – 1951, $250.00.
Private collection.

13" composition Royal Doll in suitcase box with extra wardrobe, all original, circa 1930s, $300.00.
Photo Bob Trowbridge,
Mary Lu Trowbridge collection.

20" composition Monica from Monica Studios, has rooted human hair, blue painted eyes, rosy cheeks, original long dress, circa late 1940s, $375.00. *Courtesy Odis Gregg.*

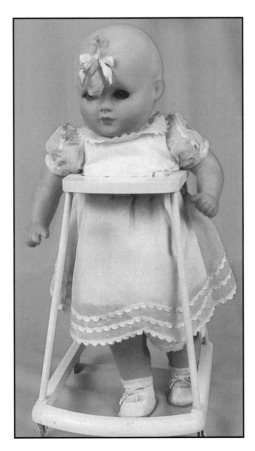

14" composition mechanical Italian walking doll, hazel sleep eyes, closed mouth, lightly molded hair, single strand of blonde hair, heavy composition body with keywound mechanism, supported in wooden walker, circa late 1940s, $95.00. *Courtesy McMasters Doll Auctions.*

Deluxe Reading

Deluxe Reading manufactured dolls from 1957 to 1965 that were sold at supermarkets as premiums — a reward for purchasing something else or groceries totaling a certain figure. They were marketed with several names: Deluxe Premium Corp., Deluxe Reading, Deluxe Topper, Deluxe Toy Creations, Topper Corp., and Topper Toys. They were of stuffed vinyl, jointed at the neck only, with sleep eyes and rooted hair. The dolls were inexpensively dressed, often as brides or in long formals. They also made 8" vinyl Penny Brite dolls with side-glancing eyes and a vinyl carrying case.

What to look for:

More and more of these dolls are showing up, often still packed in their original box. Unfortunately those that were played with often had problems with the stuffed vinyl rupturing at the neck. The costumes or accessories on some of these dolls make them an interesting and overlooked collectible.

21" vinyl Deluxe Premium Sweet Judy with jointed body at neck, arms, legs, and torso, rooted saran hair, sleep eyes, blue dress with lace trim, blue hat, circa 1950s, $100.00. *Courtesy Diana Jenness.*

8" vinyl Deluxe Reading Penny
Bright, painted blue eyes, rooted
hair, original raincoat and umbrel-
la, circa 1963 – 1964, $18.50.
Courtesy Marcie Montgomery.

Disney

Walter Ellas Disney, was born in 1902 in the Chicago area, but grew up on a Missouri farm, and had his first art lessons at age 13. His family moved back to Chicago in 1917, and he entered the Chicago Academy of Fine Art and studied under cartoonist Leroy Gossitt. During World War I, at age 16, he was an ambulance driver in France. After the war, he worked for an advertising firm doing animation.

With his brother, Roy, Disney came to Hollywood where they set up their own animation studio, and in 1927 his first character, Oswald the Lucky rabbit, appeared in a silent cartoon series. Finding he did not own the rights to his cartoon, they were held by the distributor, Disney determined he would not lose control of his own creations again. He then created a new mouse character, first named Mortimer, but later named Mickey by his wife.

Charlotte Clark designed and made the first Mickey Mouse doll and won Disney's approval for this copyrighted character. The demand soon overcame her production capabilities and the Disney brothers asked a major toy distributor, George Borgfeldt in New York, to mass produce and market the doll. Unfortunately, these dolls proved inferior to Clark's dolls, so the Disneys got the idea to make a pattern and have people make their own dolls. McCalls offered pattern #91 to make a stuffed Mickey Mouse in 1932.

After Mickey and Minnie Mouse came Donald Duck, Pluto, Red Riding Hood, the Wolf and the Three Little Pigs and then, Snow White and the Seven Dwarfs, Cinderella, and Pinnochio. Some of the early firms who produced dolls for Disney include: Lenci and Lars of Italy, Steiff, Chad Valley, Dean's Rag, Gund, Crown, Knickerbocker, Ideal, Horsman, Borgfeldt, Krueger, and Alexander. Because Disney retained the copyright for these dolls, he demanded high quality in the production and costuming of the dolls — and defended infringement on the use of his copyrights. Disney dolls are great collectibles and their high quality has been appreciated over the years.

What to look for:

Because of the popularity of the Disney movies, cartoons, comics, and theme parks and the following explosion of related dolls sold in their gift shops, a collector could have a collection of just Disney dolls. The early cloth dolls should be clean and bright, and have original clothing. Because early cloth dolls like Mickey Mouse were so loved, they are hard to find in excellent condition, but even worn dolls have some value. These dolls still turn up in estate and garage sales — what child did not bring home a memento from their Disneyland visit.

15" cloth Knickerbocker Mickey Mouse Clown, oilcloth, pie eyes, circa 1930s, $3,100.00.
Courtesy McMasters Doll Auctions.

9" velvet all-cloth Steiff
Mickey Mouse, well worn,
circa 1930s, $400.00.
Courtesy Susan L. Chase.

15½" cloth Pinocchio, painted
features, wood articulated arms
and legs, original clothes, childhood doll, circa 1940s, $500.00.
Courtesy Linda Maddux.

11" composition Crown Toy Co. Pinocchio, all original, with hang tag, small touch up on nose, circa 1940s, $175.00.
Courtesy McMasters Doll Auctions.

12" vinyl Tinkerbell, rooted synthetic hair, painted eyes, original green felt suit, and pink plastic wings with glitter, circa 1960s, $65.00.
Courtesy Millie Busch.

12½" Seven Dwarfs, all-cloth, with painted buckram faces, name hats, circa 1938, $2,200.00.
Courtesy Amanda Hash.

Effanbee

Bernard Fleishaker and Hugo Baum formed a partnership, Fleischaker and Baum, in 1910 in New York City that would eventually be known as Effanbee. They began making rag and crude composition dolls, and even had Lenox make some bisque heads for them. They developed a very high quality composition doll with a high quality finish. This characterizes their dolls of the 1920s and 1930s and lasted until after the World War II, when the company was sold to Noma Electric. The company declined with the death of Hugo Baum in 1940, but had remarkable success with a series of dolls, including Bubbles, Grumpy, Lovums, Patsy, and Dy-Dee. Effanbee was a very entrepreneurial company during its prominent years using the talents of free-lance doll artist, Bernard Lipfert who created Bubbles, Patsy, and Dy-Dee as well as Shirley Temple for Ideal, the Dionne Quintuplets for Alexander, and Ginny for Vogue. Today, Effanbee Doll Company is owned by Stanley and Irene Wahlberg who have reintroduced many of Effanbee's 1930s favorites in vinyl, painted for a composition look.

What to look for:

Effanbee's early composition dolls are classics and the painted finish was the finest available in its day. Unfortunately, the finish on played-with dolls was prone to scuffs and bumps, not to mention that these playthings have to have been stored for 70 years or more and subject to varying degrees of heat, cold, and moisture. The biggest threat to composition dolls is changes in relative humidity. When the humidity is over 85 percent, conditions are ripe for the growth of bacteria that causes the paint to decompose, flake, or peel. Also avoid direct sunlight to minimize fading. It is necessary to keep composition dolls clean and in a stable environment. Composition dolls should be clean, with rosy cheeks, costumed in original or appropriate costumes. These were some of the greatest dolls of the composition era and a treasure when you find them.

Later hard plastic and vinyl dolls also have problems with cleanliness and high relative humidity. You can, however, still find all-original dolls with labeled or tagged costumes and good color and condition.

Composition

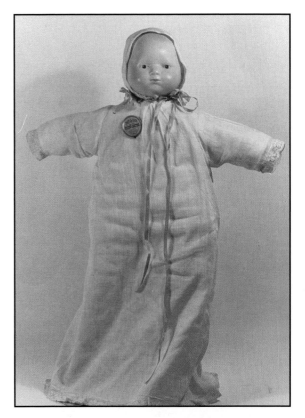

14" composition Pat-O-Pat newborn baby with cloth body containing mechanism that when squeezed allows hands to clap, wears original pinback button, $325.00.

Private collection.

Effanbee

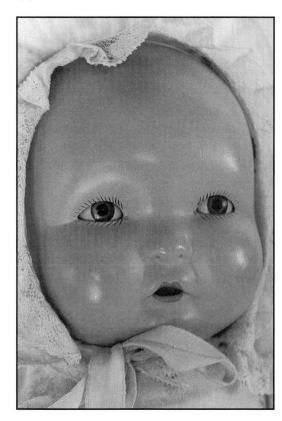

16" composition Lamkin character baby with flange neck, sleep eyes, cloth body, molded ring on finger, realistically shaped feet, redressed, circa 1931, $350.00. *Private collection.*

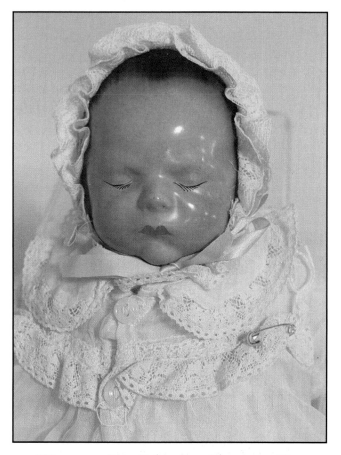

13" composition Babyette with composition hands, painted molded hair, sleeping baby with sleep eyes, cloth body, arms, and legs, introduced in 1945 Montgomery Wards catalog, all original, $495.00. *Courtesy Chantal Jeschien.*

11" composition Grumpy in original felt outfit, painted features, heavily molded hair, circa 1912, $295.00. *Courtesy June Algeier.*

15" black composition
Grumpykins, painted
side-glancing eyes, cloth body,
crier, original outfit, some paint
flaking, circa 1927+, $350.00.
Courtesy Janet Hill.

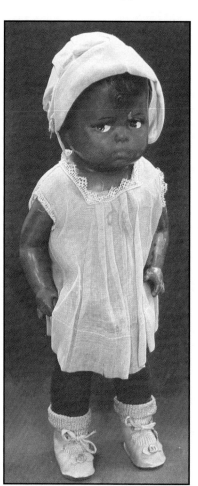

12" composition Grumpykins dolls dressed as
Amish couple, some flaking, *Effanbee
Dolls//Walk, Talk Sleep,* tagged Pennsylvania
Dutch Dolls by Marie Polack, $175.00 pair.
Courtesy McMasters Doll Auctions.

21" composition mama doll
with composition shoulder
plate, tin sleep eyes, mohair
wig over molded hair, closed
mouth, cloth body with
crier, swing legs, original
labeled costume, metal heart
necklace, circa 1923,
$500.00.
Courtesy Marian Pettygrove.

Effanbee

19" composition Rosemary, red mohair wig, re-dressed in old clothes, circa 1926, $325.00. *Courtesy Betty Jane Fronefield.*

17" composition Baby Dainty, all original mama doll, mohair wig, with flirty eyes, shown in 1930 Montgomery Ward catalog, $300.00. *Courtesy Betty Jane Fronefield.*

25" composition Rosemary, human hair wig, blue tin eyes, original chain necklace, circa 1925, $435.00. *Private collection.*

21" composition American Child, original coat, one glove, human hair wig, light crazing, circa 1939+, $525.00.
Courtesy McMasters Doll Auctions.

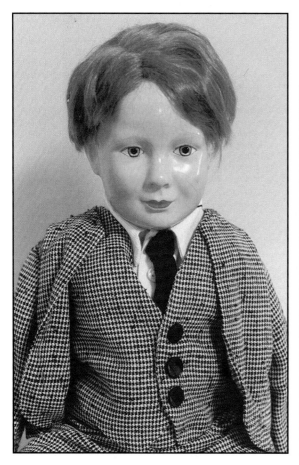

17½" composition American Children boy by Dewees Cochran, painted features, mohair wig, nicely dressed, circa 1936 – 1939, $1,300.00.
Courtesy Amanda Hash.

Effanbee

18" composition Little Lady purchased as all original, blue sleep eyes, rosebud mouth, brown human hair wig, fully jointed body, circa 1939 – 1942, $200.00. *Courtesy Iva Mae Jones.*

14½" composition Little Lady, marked *ANNE SHIRLEY* on torso, human hair wig, mint with box, hang tag, metal bracelet, circa 1939, $500.00. *Photo Bob Trowbridge, Mary Lu Trowbridge collection.*

14" composition Little Lady, human hair wig, sleep eyes, risqué in bra, panties, and peignoir, circa 1940s, $275.00. *Courtesy Bev Mitchell.*

15" composition Little Lady, marked *Anne-Shirley* on back, paper heart tag, *I Am Little Lady, An Effanbee Durable Doll,* all original, complete with box, circa 1939+, $365.00.
Courtesy McMasters Doll Auctions.

21" composition Little Lady dolls with gold metal heart tags, original outfits, circa 1939+, $350.00+ each.
Courtesy Gay Smedes.

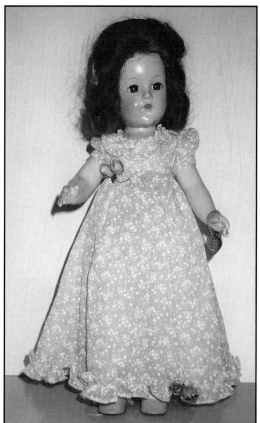

15" composition Little Lady with metal heart bracelet, human hair wig, marked *Effan-bee//Anne Shirley,* circa 1939 – 1940s, $300.00.
Courtesy Dee Cermak.

Effanbee

18" composition Little Lady with original dress, human hair wig, crazed sleep eyes, circa 1940s, $175.00.
Courtesy Dolores Jesurun.

21" composition Little Lady with original pink checked dress, human hair wig, sleep eyes, circa 1940s, $450.00.
Courtesy Sheryl Wetenkamp.

8½" composition Butin-nose ethnic pair, in original costume, gold paper hang tag on girl, circa 1936+, $500.00 for the pair.
Courtesy Dee Cermak.

8" composition Butin-nose
dressed in original ethnic
costume, possibly Turkish,
circa 1936, $225.00.
Courtesy Janet Hill.

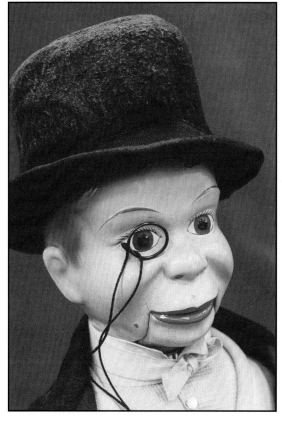

20" composition Charlie McCarthy, all
original with black tuxedo, pinback button,
painted brown eyes, hinged ventriloquist
mouth, circa 1937, $525.00.
Courtesy Odis Gregg.

14" composition Suzanne,
human hair wig, all original
with lovely cheek color, circa
1940, $300.00.
Courtesy Betty Jane Fronefield.

Effanbee

14" composition Suzanne in original
pink and white dress, sleep eyes,
human hair wig, metal heart bracelet,
lovely coloring, circa 1940, $325.00.
Courtesy Joanne Morgan.

19½" composition Little Lady, all original
with box, circa 1936, $650.00.
Photo Bob Trowbridge, Mary Lu Trowbridge collection.

Two 12" composition Portrait
Dolls Bride and Groom, circa
1949, $600.00 for pair.
Courtesy Irene Grundtvig.

Vinyl and Hard Plastic

14" hard plastic Tintair, circa 1951, $400.00. *Courtesy McMasters Doll Auctions.*

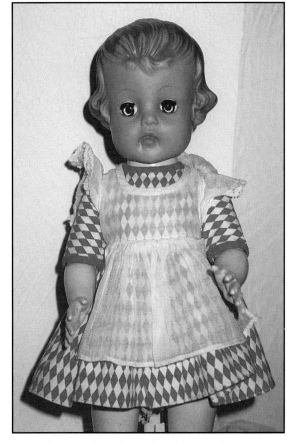

14" vinyl girl with molded hair, sleep eyes, hard plastic body, original outfit, circa 1950s, $35.00. *Courtesy Bev Mitchell.*

8" vinyl Scarecrow designed by Faith Wick, all original, mint-in-box, circa 1983, $100.00 each. *Courtesy Sue Kinkade.*

Effanbee

17" all-vinyl Suzie Sunshine in Effanbee's Yesterday Collection, rooted hair, sleep eyes, fully jointed, circa 1977, $50.00. *Courtesy Cathie Clark.*

18" vinyl Suzie Sunshine from the Over the Rainbow Collection, played with, circa 1973, $35.00. *Courtesy Bev Mitchell.*

16" vinyl Gum Drop, original outfit, rooted hair, sleep eyes, vinyl body, circa 1962 – 1967 and 1970 – 1972, $49.00. *Courtesy Cathy Chesnut.*

Bubbles

One of the great early composition dolls that was designed by Bernard Lipfert and made by Effanbee was Bubbles, first advertised in *Playthings* in 1926. First made in the 21" size, it soon had nine or more sizes available. Bubbles was a sensation, with molded blonde hair, sleep eyes, open mouth, sturdy cloth body with bent cloth legs, and composition arms.

As with any doll that sells well in the toy market, imitations soon follow, and Effanbee filed a lawsuit against Horsman, for one. One of the things Bernard Lipfert who designed most of the American dolls in the 1920s, 1930s, and 1940s, learned was how to change each doll just enough to satisfy the courts that the new doll was different. Working independently on commission for many companies, Lipfert was a master at doll design.

One of the attractive features about Bubbles was the modeling of the hands which allowed the doll to pose with one finger towards its mouth. Bubbles was made in a few black versions and later as a toddler. Bubbles came with a round paper name tag and also a metal heart necklace and was advertised as the doll with the golden heart. Variations with painted eyes and composition shoulder plates have been noted. Original costumes included a white bonnet with big stand-up ruffle, long white cotton christening dresses, and brushed wool jackets and caps, and short silk dresses and hats. Costumes carry the red oval Effanbee Bubbles cloth tag.

25" composition Bubbles, all original with labeled box, marked on shoulder plate *Effanbee//Bubbles//Copr.1924//Made in USA*, circa 1924+, $750.00. *Courtesy Irene Grundtvig.*

The Patsy Family

Another one of Effanbee's great success stories was the Patsy doll designed by Bernard Lipfert and advertised in 1928. She almost was not named Patsy. Identical ads advertised her as Mimi late in 1927 and then as Patsy in 1928 *Playthings* magazines. Patsy was one of the first dolls to have a wardrobe manufactured just for her by Effanbee and other manufacturers. She was made of all-composition and her patent was hotly defended by Effanbee. What was actually patented was a neck joint that allowed the doll to pose and stand alone. She portrayed a three-year-old girl with short bobbed red hair with a molded headband, painted side-glancing eyes, pouty mouth, bent right arm, and she wore simple classic dresses closed with a safety pin. She had a golden heart charm bracelet and/or a gold paper heart tag with her name. Patsy was so popular she soon had several sisters, many variations, and even a boyfriend, Skippy.

Effanbee promoted Patsy sales with a newspaper *The Patsytown News* that went to a reported quarter million children. Effanbee also had an Aunt Patsy who toured the country promoting their dolls. In addition, it formed a Patsy Doll Club and gave free pinback membership buttons to children who wrote in or bought a Patsy doll. Effanbee tied its doll line to popular current events such as producing George and Martha Washington for the bicentennial of George's birth. The company costumed a group of dolls like the *White Horse Inn* operetta that toured the U.S. During the war years, Effanbee fashioned military uniforms for the Skippy dolls and also costumed dolls in ethnic dress (Dutch) or after characters in books like *Alice in Wonderland*.

The death of Hugo Baum in 1940 and the loss of income during the war years threw Effanbee into a decline. In 1946, Effanbee was sold to Noma Electric who reissued a 1946 Patsy and later a new 17" Patsy Joan. Effanbee has changed owners several times. Stanley and Irene Wahlberg reissued vinyl Patsy family dolls during the 1990s. Effanbee again has new management in 1999. Limited editions of Patsy Ann and Skippy dolls were issued during the 1970s, and Patsy reappeared in vinyl in the 1980s. Effanbee reissued Patsy Joan in 1995, and are continuing in 1996, 1997, and 1998 with a new group of Patsy, Skippy, and Wee Patsy dolls in vinyl painted to look like the old composition ones. These are already becoming collectibles for the modern collector.

Babies

Left: 11" composition black Patsy Baby with metal heart bracelet *Effanbee Patsy Baby Kin* **side-glancing eyes, three black string pigtails tied with red ribbons, $400.00; Right: 11" composition Patsy Baby, green sleep eyes, closed mouth, bent-limb baby body, $190.00; circa 1931.** *Courtesy McMasters Doll Auctions.*

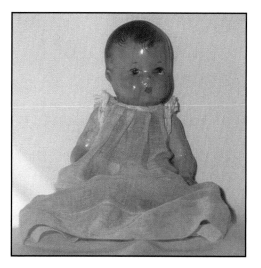

6½" composition Patsy Baby
Tinyette in original gown and dia-
per, circa 1934, $250.00.
Courtesy Gay Smedes.

9½" composition Patsy Baby twins in original
clothes and bunting blanket, with painted eyes,
one brown, one blue, excellent condition, circa
1931, $695.00. *Courtesy Millie Carol.*

10½" composition Patsy Baby twins, cloth
bodies, celluloid hands, World War II era,
$500.00 for pair.
Courtesy Maxine Jackson.

9" composition twin Patsy Babyettes, blue sleep eyes, original blue and white cotton outfits, excellent condition, circa 1932, $600.00+ for pair.
Courtesy Lilian Booth.

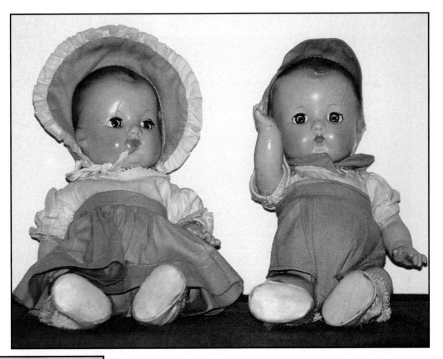

9" composition Patsy Babyette pair, sleep eyes, painted molded hair, in original navy blue outfits, circa 1932, $650.00 for pair. *Courtesy Gay Smedes.*

9" composition Patsy Babyette Tousle Tots, sleep eyes, closed mouths, molded hair under original skin wigs, composition bent-limb baby bodies, pink/white striped pajamas, all original, circa 1941, $400.00.
Courtesy McMasters Doll Auctions.

9" composition Patsy Babyette twins
with caracul reddish blonde wigs,
original flannel pajamas and robes,
excellent condition, circa 1933,
$600.00+ for pair.
Courtesy Lilian Booth.

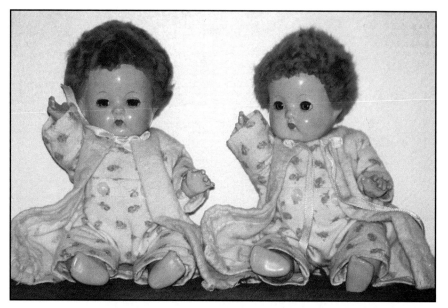

Child

13" composition early Patsy marked
EFFANBEE//PATSY in oval on back of
shoulder plate, cloth body with crier,
painted molded hair, circa 1920s,
$175.00. *Photo Bob Trowbridge, Mary Lu
Trowbridge collection.*

5½" composition Wee Patsy twins, painted blue
eyes, closed mouths, painted molded hair, composition child bodies jointed at shoulders and hips,
painted molded socks and shoes, original outfits,
circa 1935, $375.00.
Courtesy McMasters Doll Auctions.

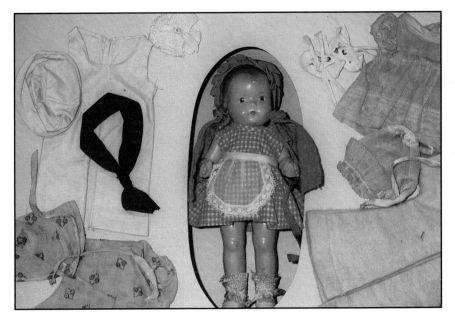

6" composition Wee Patsy, painted molded hair and features,
painted shoes and socks, re-
dressed in copy of original dress,
circa 1935+, $300.00.
Courtesy Gay Smedes.

8" composition Patsy Baby Tinyette toddler dressed as Red Riding
Hood in trunk with wardrobe, excellent condition, circa 1934,
$750.00+. *Courtesy Lilian Booth.*

8" composition Tinyette toddlers Kit and Kat,
dressed in original Dutch outfits with wood-
en shoes, circa 1935, $800.00 for pair.
Courtesy McMasters Doll Auctions.

9" composition Hawaiian Patsyette in
original grass skirt, print bodice, paper lei
and head, wrist, and ankle bands, circa
1931+, $950.00.
Courtesy McMasters Doll Auctions.

9½" rare composition Patsyette Hawaiian queen, all original with box, with Liberty House in Honolulu card, circa 1930s, $1,000.00. *Private collection.*

9" composition Patsyette, complete with original box, dressed in red and white checked dress, white leatherette tie shoes, navy blue felt coat, circa 1931, $800.00. *Courtesy McMasters Doll Auctions.*

11" composition black Patsykins, glassene eyes, closed mouth, composition body, circa 1931, $600.00; 8" Baby Tinyette Toddler, painted eyes and hair, closed mouth, circa 1935, $185.00. *Courtesy McMasters Doll Auctions.*

Effanbee

Left: 11½" composition black Patsykins, marked *Patsykin* on head and *Patsy Jr.* on back, dress is tagged *Effanbee Durable Dolls, made in U.S.A.,* bracelet reads *Effanbee Patsy Kin* circa 1931, $700.00; Right: 11" composition Patsykins marked *Effanbee, Patsy Jr.* doll on back, *Effanbee Durable Dolls* on dress tag and on bracelet, circa 1931, $575.00. *Courtesy McMasters Doll Auctions.*

11½" composition Patsy Jr., replaced dress is a copy of old pattern with old material, circa 1931+, $250.00. *Courtesy Gay Smedes.*

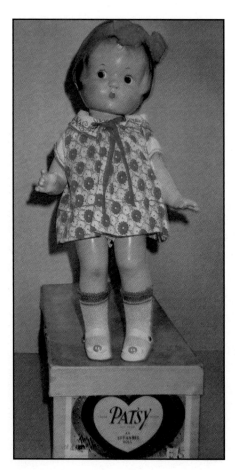

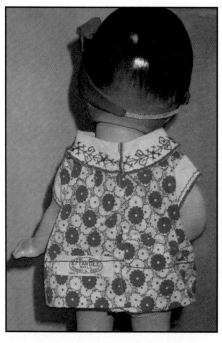

14" composition Patsy marked *EFFANBEE//PATSY//PAT. PEND.//DOLL,* all original tagged dress with box, circa 1928+, $600.00. *Courtesy Irene Grundtvig.*

14" composition Patsy with sleep eyes, human hair wig, metal heart bracelet, original yellow silk dress and teddy, circa 1933+, $400.00.
Courtesy Gay Smedes.

16" composition Patsy Joan in original red checked outfit, red shoes and socks, with extra wardrobe, circa 1931, $750.00.
Courtesy Lilian Booth.

16" composition Patsy Joan, sleep eyes, mohair wig, original dress, replaced shoes and socks, circa 1931+, $400.00.
Courtesy Gay Smedes.

16" composition Patsy Joan, brown sleep eyes/lashes, closed rose-bud mouth, mohair wig over unpainted molded hair, five-piece composition body, metal heart bracelet, circa 1931, $575.00.
Courtesy McMasters Doll Auctions.

13½" composition Patsy with blue painted eyes, brown painted molded hair, wears old, perhaps original, outfit, circa 1928, $375.00.
Courtesy Dee Cermak.

14" composition Patsy in green outfit, circa 1928, $375.00.
Courtesy Jane Foster.

19" composition Patsy Ann with her trunk and complete wardrobe, all-composition with human hair wig, circa 1929, $900.00.
Courtesy McMasters Doll Auctions.

19" composition Patsy Ann pair in original cotton print outfits, circa 1929, $400.00 each. *Courtesy Jane Foster.*

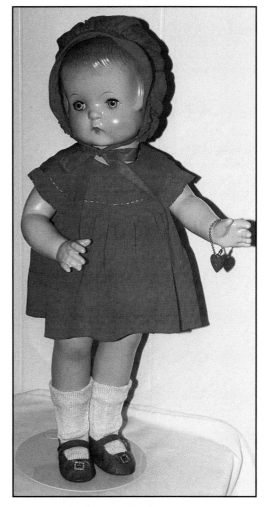

19" composition Patsy Ann in original tagged red silk dress and red leatherette shoes, circa 1929+, $600.00. *Courtesy Marian Pettygrove.*

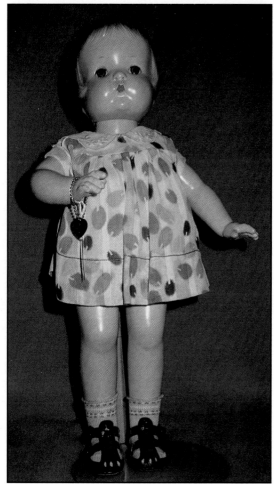

19" composition Patsy Ann in original balloon print dress, new shoes, circa 1929, $650.00. *Courtesy Millie Carol.*

Effanbee

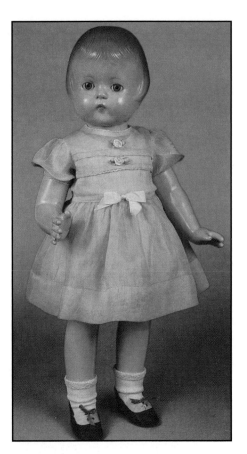

22" all-composition Patsy Lou marked on her back, *EFFANBEE//PATSY LOU,* green sleep eyes, painted molded bobbed hair, original pink organdy dress, light crazing, circa 1931+, $525.00. *Courtesy McMasters Doll Auctions.*

22" composition Patsy Lou, clear green eyes, painted molded bobbed hair, old dress, circa 1931, $500.00. *Courtesy McMasters Doll Auctions.*

22" composition Patsy Lou, mohair wig, sleep eyes, nice color, metal heart bracelet, original clothes, circa 1931, $550.00. *Courtesy Janet Hill.*

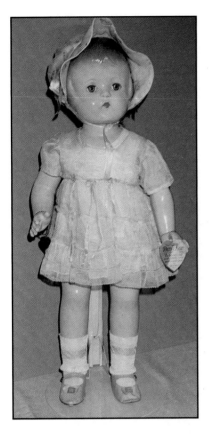

22" composition Patsy Lou with rare metal name bracelet that reads *Effanbee Patsy Lou* and paper heart tag, tagged dress, with matching hat, circa 1932, $600.00.
Courtesy Betty Jane Fronefield.

26" all-composition Patricia Ruth marked *Patsy Ruth* on the head, human hair wig, sleep eyes, closed mouth, copy of original silk dress, circa 1935, $3,600.00.
Courtesy McMasters Doll Auctions.

15" composition Patsy/Patricia variant, blue painted eyes with sideways hearts, original dress, magnets in hands to hold metal accessories, circa 1940s, $400.00.
Courtesy Betty Jane Fronefield.

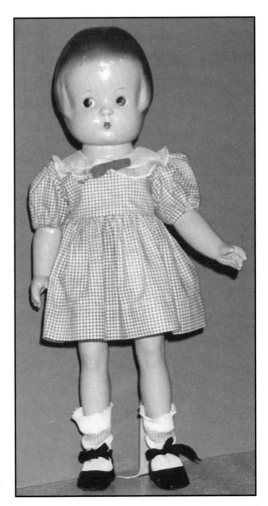

Effanbee

30" composition Patsy Mae, brown
sleep eyes, closed rosebud mouth,
original human hair wig, cloth body
with composition arms and legs,
circa 1934, $1,300.00.
Courtesy McMasters Doll Auctions.

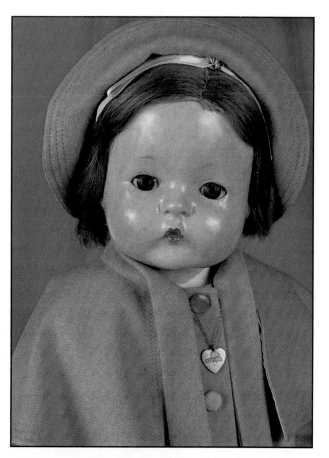

30" composition Patsy Mae, composition head
and shoulder plate, cloth body, composition
arms and legs, brown sleep eyes, human hair
wig, circa 1934, $1,350.00.
Courtesy McMasters Doll Auctions.

14" composition Skippy Aviator,
painted eyes and hair, cloth body,
circa 1940, $3,200.00; 11" composi-
tion Patricia Kin, tin sleep eyes,
closed mouth, human hair wig, circa
1935, $1,100.00.
Courtesy McMasters Doll Auctions.

14" composition Skippy in soldier uniform, painted blue eyes, brown painted molded hair, molded shoes, marked *Effanbee//Skippy//C.//P.L. Crosby,* circa 1940s, $550.00.
Courtesy Dee Cermak.

14" composition black Skippy Soldier, painted brown eyes to side, closed mouth, painted molded hair, cloth body, composition arms and legs, original army uniform, replaced tie and belt, circa 1940s, $1,350.00.
Courtesy McMasters Doll Auctions.

14" composition Skippy in military uniform and advertised only as Soldier, with gold paper hang tag, magnets in hands, box, circa 1940s, $750.00.
Courtesy Sharon Kolibaba.

14" composition Skippy with magnets in hands to hold accessories, molded black shoes, cloth body, original sailor costume, should have white hat, circa 1940s, $300.00.
Courtesy Millie Carol.

Effanbee

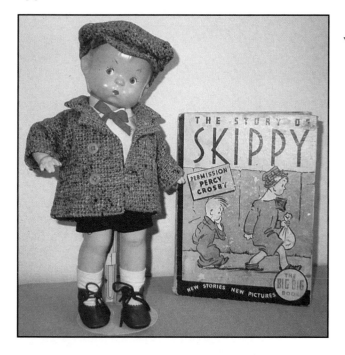

14" all-composition Skippy with painted features, painted molded hair, re-dressed, circa 1929, $350.00. *Courtesy Peggy Viskocil.*

14" composition Skippy Tyrolean Boy, painted eyes and hair, closed mouth, composition body, circa 1936, $800.00; 6" Wee Patsy in Fairy Princess Case, original, circa 1935, $725.00. *Courtesy McMasters Doll Auctions.*

14" composition Skippy with composition arms and legs, cloth body, painted molded socks and shoes, in policeman's costume, no hat, gun in hoster, circa 1929, $475.00. *Photo, Scott Gladden, courtesy Ellen Sturgess.*

15" composition Patricia as
Martha Washington in fancy
dress, replaced lace and
bows, white mohair wig,
circa 1935+, $400.00+.
Courtesy Pat Schuda.

15" composition Patricia as Martha
Washington, green eyes, all original,
circa 1935, $500.00. *Private collection.*

15" composition Patricia in Anne
Shirley movie costume, brown
mohair wig, circa 1935+, $450.00.
Courtesy Gay Smedes.

Effanbee

14" composition Patsy, painted molded eyes and hair, head turns and tilts, arms and legs jointed, dressed in pink checked cotton with embroidered organdy ruffle at shoulders, matching bonnet, circa 1946, $350.00.
Courtesy Iva Mae Jones.

14" composition Patsy, painted eyes, molded hair, unmarked, original red checked sundress, circa 1946, $400.00.
Courtesy Gay Smedes.

14" composition Patsy, circa 1946, $375.00.
Courtesy Millie Carol.

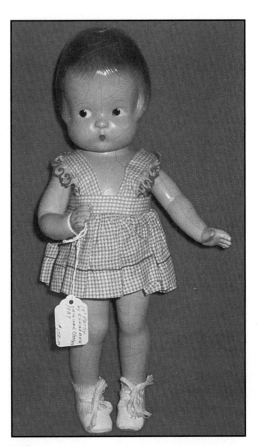

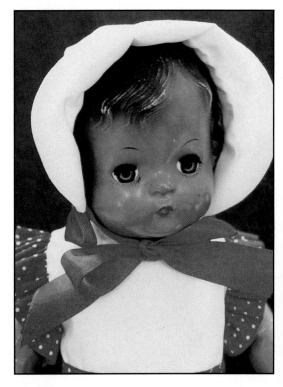

17" composition black Patsy Joan re-dressed in copy of original dress, painted molded hair, brown sleep eyes, some paint rubs, circa 1946, $275.00.
Courtesy Stella May Baylis.

Dy-Dee, "The Almost Human Doll"

Effanbee contracted with Marie Whitman who developed a drink/wet valve mechanism. Effanbee used the talents of Bernard Lipfert to sculpt a doll head with molded ears that was to be made of hard rubber and contracted the bodies out to Miller Rubber Co. of Akron, Ohio. The idea of a doll wetting its diaper was considered in poor taste and the doll was rejected by Harrods in London, until one of the royal family requested one.

The doll was referred to as the "Almost Human Doll" in promotions. The doll was introduced in April of 1934 in two sizes. It soon was available with layettes and trunks, or dolls, wardrobes, and layettes could be purchased separately. By 1935, Dy-Dees dolls came in several sizes, 11" Dy-Dee-Ette, 13" Dy-Dee-Kin, 15" Dy-Dee, and 20" Dy-Dee Ann, that soon became Dy-Dee Lou. Aunt Patsy was the official spokesperson on Dy-Dee care.

In 1936, there was a new Golden Treasure Chest to hold Dy-Dee's wardrobe as well as a bassinette to bathe her and a buggy to carry her places. An instruction booklet was now included with Dy-Dee titled, "What Every Young Doll Mother Should Know."

The book *Dy-Dee Doll's Days* was featured in Dy-Dee sets in the 1937 Ward's Catalog. New accessories included a diaper bag and mother outfit, which included a rubber apron, a white cotton uniform cap and apron, bath accessories, hot water bottle, and diary.

In 1938, Dy-Dee could blow Bubbles with her bubble-pipe and sip from her spoon. A new size was the 9" Dy-Dee-Wee. Queen Holden drew Dy-Dee Baby paper dolls that were published by Whitman. In 1939, advertising showed pink and blue name print pajamas with the Dy-Dee sets.

In 1940, Dy-Dee was redesigned to include applied rubber ears and real nostrils with holes. Cotton swabs to clean the ears and nose came with Dy-Dee sets. There were three sizes of Dy-Dees, 11", 15", and 20".

In 1941 the 20" Dy-Dee Lou's name was changed to Dy-Dee Louise, and Dy-Dee Jane was the 15" doll and Dy-Dee Ellen was 11" tall. New, too, were blankets with Dy-Dee name print. The tousle head caracul wig was new that year. Dy-Dee dolls with striped pajamas are seen in the ads. During the war years Dy-Dee was featured with layettes and bassinettes and as the war progressed and rubber shortages appeared, just accessories were promoted, not the dolls.

In 1946, Effanbee was sold to Noma Electric and they began offering Dy-Dee in a travel type case with handle and lock. New, was bubble bath in the layette. In 1948, a crier/pacifier was included in the layette and after 1948 tear ducts were added. Dy-Dee was produced in hard plastic and vinyl in the 1950s.

What to look for:

Look for Dy-Dee dolls in good condition, without all the color scrubbed off by some loving owner who may have put her doll in a bassinette, or allowed water from her drink bottle to leak onto her face. Dy-Dee dolls had wonderful wardrobe trunks and layette sets and some are still available as well as accessories such as bottles, bubble pipes, diaries, and bathinettes. Many have deteriorating bodies because the rubber may have cracked or heat has caused it to go out of shape. Some can be stuffed with cotton or covered with stockings if they are flaking. Still a wonderful collectible.

Effanbee

15" hard rubber Dy-Dee Baby, applied ears, complete with labeled box and all accessories, circa 1940+, $400.00. *Courtesy McMasters Doll Auctions.*

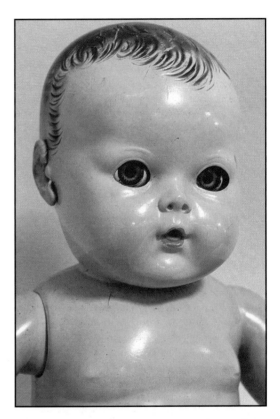

19½" rubber Dy-Dee Lou with applied ears, painted molded hair, sleep eyes, open mouth, rubber drink and wet baby body, nude, excellent condition, usually the rubber has dried out and hardened, circa 1940s, $350.00. *Courtesy Linda Maddux.*

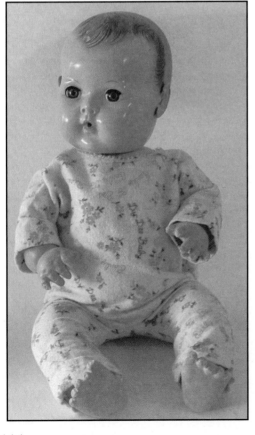

15" hard rubber Dy-Dee Baby with applied ears, sleep eyes, painted molded hair, open mouth for bottle, original name print pajamas, drink and wet flexible rubber baby body, good condition, circa 1940s, $225.00. *Private collection.*

20" hard plastic Dy-Dee Lou
with tear ducts and tousel
wig, circa 1950s, $395.00.
Courtesy Pam Martinec.

11" hard plastic Dy-Dee Ellen, applied rubber ears, sleep eyes, drink wet feature, tear
ducts, original coat and bonnet, circa 1956,
$125.00. *Courtesy Micki Beston.*

Ethnic Dolls

Collectors sometimes refer to dolls dressed in regional or national costumes as ethnic or tourist dolls as they were commonly available in shops visited by tourists looking for a souvenir. Dolls dressed in national costume at times were touted as "educational" by showing the costume or dress of that country.

Today some collectors are trying to identify many of these ethnic dolls which are often quite charming and passed over for the better-known collectible dolls. One doll club has taken on the project researching certain groups of dolls. After one year's study, they became so engrossed, they decided to continue for another year. This is an area with little research and is well worth continued interest. Dolls in national costume were made of many mediums, including bisque, cloth, composition, hard plastic, and vinyl. During the 1930s, 1940s, 1950s, and later, many dolls dressed in regional costumes could be purchased cheaply as souvenirs in different areas. A wide variety of these dolls are unmarked or made by little known companies. This category is sometimes a catchall for dolls that have little history and no category. Many were cheaply made and mass produced for the tourist market, but some were extremely well made and are whimsical and charming and make an interesting and eclectic collection.

What to look for:

The workmanship and the costuming make these dolls valuable. Look for clean, all original dolls with boxes, labels, and/or tagged clothing. Try for dolls with very well-made clothing that is clean, has bright colors, no fading or soil. This category has big potential for collectors as it is not as popular with older collectors, who seek more conventional dolls in ethnic costumes. Acquire dolls that are appealing to you, but always look for well-made dolls of good color and original costume.

9½" celluloid Austrian pair with painted features, molded hair, regional costumes, tagged Zellertal with house logo, after 1960, $200.00 for pair.
Courtesy Marcie Montgomery.

7" clay Jay Irish lady, felt body over wire armature, $45.00.
Courtesy Cherie Gervais.

12" composition Jay of Dublin Sligo 1830 woman with felt over wire armature body, handmade clothing, skirt tucked up to show petticoat, good attention to detail, red hang tag, circa 1970s, $55.00.
Private collection.

12" composition Jay of Dublin Connemara Man with felt over wire armature body, handmade clothing with good attention to detail, red hang tag, circa 1970s, $55.00. *Private collection.*

8½" painted hard plastic doll, Lenci-type, mint-in-box, marked *Bambola Mignon Terni*, dark dress, pink apron, circa 1950s – 1960s, $35.00.
Courtesy Joanne Morgan.

8½" painted hard plastic doll, Lenci-type, mint-in-box, marked *Bambola Mignon Liquria*, white blouse, pink and yellow skirt, white apron, circa 1950s – 1960s, $35.00.
Courtesy Joanne Morgan.

8½" painted hard plastic doll, Lenci-type, mint-in-box, marked *Bambola Mignon Val Gardena*, white blouse, apron, pink skirt, circa 1950s – 1960s, $35.00.
Courtesy Joanne Morgan.

13" celluloid pair in regional costume, Yugoslavia, circa 1960s, $75.00 pair.
Courtesy Martha L. Metz.

14" wooden Mexican Macho with painted features, floss hair, covered wire body, original costume, tagged *Creaciones "Cari" Mexico,* circa 1940s, $40.00.
Courtesy Carol Bennett.

11½" celluloid doll, glass eyes, mohair wig, in well made Norwegian costume, cloth body, circa 1930s, $225.00.
Courtesy Sharon Kolibaba.

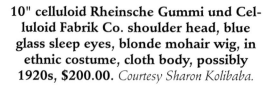

10" celluloid Rheinsche Gummi und Celluloid Fabrik Co. shoulder head, blue glass sleep eyes, blonde mohair wig, in ethnic costume, cloth body, possibly 1920s, $200.00. *Courtesy Sharon Kolibaba.*

10" celluloid German girl in ethnic costume, and 9½" hard plastic tagged *Guar* boy with molded hair, painted features in Tyrolean costume, circa 1960+, $140.00 each.
Courtesy Marcie Montgomery.

Baitz

The Baitz firm first started in Germany in 1912. After World War II, the firm moved to Austria where it became Camillo Gardtner and Company in 1963. It is still producing well-made dolls dressed in regional costumes.

Baitz dolls are 9" tall and the head appears to be painted hard plastic or composition. Since Coleman's *Collector's Encyclopedia of Dolls* refers to composition as "made of various ingredients," most collectors equate the term composition with heads made from recipes of wood pulp mixtures.

Baitz dolls are very appealing with their side-glancing painted brown eyes, open round surprise or kissing mouth, and attractive costumes. They have single-line painted eyebrows, and two brown eyelashes painted from the upper corner of the eye. They have glued-on mohair wigs with curls or braids for the girls and short hair for the boys. Their bodies are felt-over-wire armature with simple mitt felt hands. They have a red and black heart-shaped paper hang tag with BAITZ on it. On the back of the hang tag is a gold foil sticker that reads *Made in Austria* and the name of the doll or region it represents. They come in cream floral pattern boxes also with a gold foil sticker. The clothing is cotton with felt used for accent and hats. All dolls have hats or some headdress. The feet have simple black gathered cloth shoes and white cotton knit stockings. The clothing does not have fasteners or openings for removal. They come dressed both as boys and girls.

9" hard plastic Baitz Luzern girl, painted features, mohair wig, side-glancing eyes, round open/closed mouth, felt over wire body, original regional outfit, Baitz heart tag, sticker *Made in Austria* circa 1970s, $75.00.
Private collection.

9" hard plastic Baitz Appenzell boy, painted features, mohair wig, side-glancing eyes, round open/closed mouth, felt over wire body, original regional outfit, Baitz heart tag, sticker *Made in Austria,* circa 1970s, $75.00. *Private collection.*

9" hard plastic Baitz Tessin girl, painted features, mohair wig, side-glancing eyes, round open/closed mouth, felt over wire body, original regional outfit, Baitz heart tag, sticker *Made in Austria,* circa 1970s, $75.00. *Private collection.*

9" hard plastic Baitz Zorich girl, painted features, mohair wig, side-glancing eyes, round open/closed mouth, felt over wire body, original regional outfit, Baitz heart tag, sticker *Made in Austria,* circa 1970s, $75.00. *Private collection.*

9" hard plastic Baitz Hessen boy, painted features, mohair wig, side-glancing eyes, round open/closed mouth, felt over wire body, original regional outfit, Baitz heart tag, sticker *Made in Austria,* circa 1970s, $75.00. *Private collection.*

9" hard plastic Baitz Hansl boy, painted features, mohair wig, side-glancing eyes, round open/closed mouth, felt over wire body, original regional outfit, Baitz heart tag, sticker *Made in Austria,* circa 1970s, $75.00. *Private collection*.

9" hard plastic Baitz Rosl girl, painted features, mohair wig, side-glancing eyes, round open/closed mouth, felt over wire body, original regional outfit, Baitz heart tag, sticker *Made in Austria,* circa 1970s, $75.00. *Private collection.*

Ethnic Dolls

9" painted hard plastic Baitz girl in regional outfit, missing hang tag, circa 1970s, $35.00. *Courtesy Fran Fabian.*

9" painted hard plastic Baitz boy in Tyrolean outfit, missing hang tag, circa 1970s, $35.00. *Courtesy Fran Fabian.*

9" hard plastic Baitz Tegernsee girl, painted features, mohair wig, side-glancing eyes, round open/closed mouth, felt over wire body, original regional outfit, Baitz heart tag, sticker *Made in Austria,* circa 1970s, $75.00. *Private collection.*

9" hard plastic Baitz Hias boy, painted features, mohair wig, side-glancing eyes, round open/closed mouth, felt over wire body, original regional outfit, Baitz heart tag, sticker *Made in Austria,* circa 1970s, $75.00. *Private collection.*

9" hard plastic Baitz Waadt girl, painted features, mohair wig, side-glancing eyes, round open/closed mouth, felt over wire body, original regional outfit, Baitz heart tag, sticker *Made in Austria,* circa 1970s, $75.00. *Private collection.*

French Ethnic

Petticollin produced celluloid dolls for various companies that dressed them in regional costumes. Madame Le Minor, a French designer, bought dolls of composition and celluloid and costumed them selling them under her label. Other companies copied her costumed dolls from different regions of France.

16" French celluloid, painted features, mohair wig, with triangular tag marked *Poupee Reene D'Orior,* **metallic thread on clothing, circa 1950s, $150.00.**
Courtesy Irma Cook.

16" French celluloid, painted features, mohair wig, with triangular tag marked *Poupee Reene D'Orior,* **metallic thread on clothing, circa 1950s, $150.00.**
Courtesy Irma Cook.

Skookums, 1914 – 1950+

Skookums was designed and patented by Mary McAboy in 1914. The first doll heads were reported to be made of dried apples, then composition and later plastic. They were manufactured first as a cottage industry for the Denver H.H. Tammen Company and then by Arrow Novelty Co. They had side-glancing painted eyes, molded and painted features, horsehair wigs, and padded cloth over stick bodies which was formed by wrapping and folding an Indian blanket to suggest arms. The label on the bottom of the flat wooden feet reads *Trade Mark Registered (Bully Good) Indian//U.S.A.//Patented.* Later dolls had plastic molded feet. Dolls range in size from 6" to 36" store displays. Typical figures represent a chief, squaw with papoose, and child. The dolls were made for the tourist markets and sold through the Tammen Company catalogs and elsewhere. They are a nostalgic piece of Americana.

14" composition Skookums Chief in original marked box, with label on foot, dressed in blanket with braids and painted features, side-glancing eyes, circa 1930s – 1940s, $165.00. *Private collection.*

Ethnic Dolls

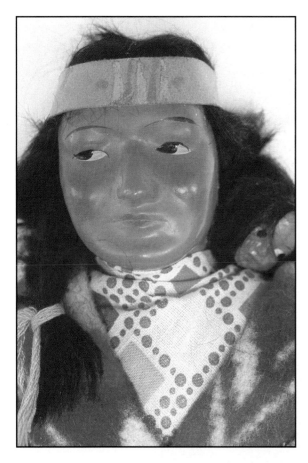

11½" composition Skookums
Squaw with papoose, wooden feet,
blanket, circa 1930s – 1940s,
$125.00. *Private collection.*

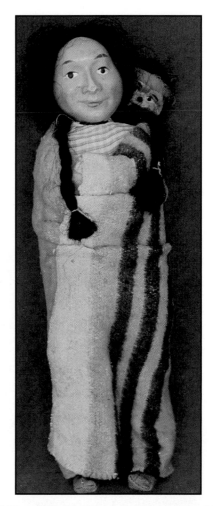

**10" celluloid Skookums Squaw with
baby, wrapped blanket forms body,
damage to celluloid head, circa
1940s, $50.00.** *Courtesy Judith Guss.*

**19½" composition Skookums Chief
with baby, designed by Mary
McAboy, blanket wrapped body,
side-glancing painted eyes, 1913+,
$475.00.** *Courtesy Debbie Crume.*

World's Fair Tourist Dolls

In Judds' *Compo Dolls, 1928 – 1985,* they report finding a 13" composition doll tagged *A Doll Craft Product.* The Judds' believe the dolls were made in the late 1930s by a factory that sold them to different marketing firms that dressed and sold them to different stores and catalog companies. It has been reported that the dolls were offered for sale at the 1939 New York World's Fair at the different pavilions representing different countries participating in the Fair.

These dolls were 8½" or 13" tall with painted side-glancing eyes, molded hair under mohair wigs, and original costumes with hang tags. The dolls are jointed all-composition with gently curved arms, pouty mouths, one line painted eyebrows, and eyelashes painted above their brown irises. A dot of white accents the right of each black pupil. The fingers are molded together and the composition is well finished, but cruder than Effanbee's Patsy family. Each has a yellow hang tag stating her name and country that her costume represents, such as "I am Katrinka from Holland," "I am Marguerita from Romania," or "I am Maria from Italy."

All-composition 13" dolls such as these with clean bright original costumes, little or no crazing, good color, complete with hang tags, in excellent condition would be priced $250.00, more if costume is elaborate or with accessories, much less if no tag, not original, or faded with heavy crazing. The 8" ones would be priced at $150.00, less for played with or soiled, depending on condition.

What to look for:

These examples of tourist dolls from the late 1939 World's Fair are charming and great collectibles. Revived interest in ethnic and tourist dolls make them a nifty collecting niche. Dolls with fine costuming with intricate details are more in demand. Look for composition dolls with little crazing, all dolls with good facial color, original costumes, hang tags, boxes, or labels. This remains a category that needs more study and research and poses a good avenue for new collectors to pursue and enjoy.

13" composition with mohair braids, painted side-glancing eyes, in ethnic costume, tagged *I am Maria from Italy,* circa 1940s, $250.00. *Courtesy Penny Pittsley.*

Ethnic Dolls

13" composition with mohair braids, painted side-glancing eyes, in ethnic costume, tagged *I am Katrinka from Holland,* circa 1939, $250.00. *Courtesy Penny Pittsley.*

13" composition with mohair braids, painted side-glancing eyes, in ethnic costume, tagged *I am Marguerita from Roumania,* circa 1939, $250.00. *Courtesy Penny Pittsley.*

8½" all-composition ethnic dolls, left to right, The
Girl of the Golden West, Scarlett, and Sonja from
Norway, circa 1939, $175.00 with tag, $125.00
without. *Courtesy Marge Meisinger.*

8½" all-composition ethnic dolls, left to right,
Sophia from Poland, Areta from Sweden, Aina
from Finland, circa 1939, $175.00 each.
Courtesy Marge Meisinger.

8½" all-composition ethnic dolls,
unmarked, no tags, circa 1939, $125.00
each. *Courtesy Marge Meisinger.*

Hard Plastic Dolls

Plastics came into use during World War II. The war and shortages of some materials caused great upheavals in the toy industry. Some plants were converted to make items for the war effort. After the war, some companies began to use plastic for dolls. Hard plastic seems to have been a good material for doll use. Relatively unbreakable, it does not deteriorate with time, as did the "magic skin" and other materials that were tried and discarded. The prime years of use, roughly a ten year period (late 1940s – 1950s), produced a wide variety of beautiful dolls that Baby Boomers still remember fondly. With the advent of vinyl, in the late 1950s and early 1960s, less hard plastic dolls were made, although occasionally some manufacturer still presents hard plastic dolls today.

What to look for:

Look for clean dolls with rosy cheek color, original clothing, labels, boxes, hang tags, or brochures. Dirt may have caused the plastic to change chemically with the growth of bacteria when the relative humidity is high. Another way for collectors to find inexpensive dolls is to look for those that are unmarked or by little known companies.

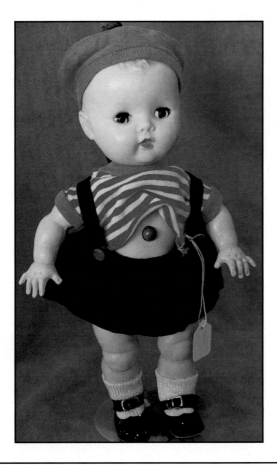

8" hard plastic Block Doll Co., Answer Doll, has button in tummy, makes head move yes or no, straight leg, non-walker, painted molded hair, circa 1951 – 1957, $95.00. *Courtesy Christine McWilliams.*

8" hard plastic Roller Skater
with unmarked box and
brochure, original outfit, circa
1940s – 1950s, $75.00.
Courtesy Annmarie Travis.

11½" hard plastic P.M.A. Dolls, Inc.
Missy with Dynel hair, sleep eyes, all
original in marked box, circa 1950s,
$75.00. *Courtesy Sue Kinkade.*

7½" hard plastic Debby Doll Mfg.
Co. Scotch Girl, all original in
marked box, circa 1950s, $25.00.
Courtesy Cleveland Atkinson.

13" hard plastic Nun doll in cathedral window box that reads, *Attend the Church of your faith at least once a week — for the Family That Prays Together — Stays Together,* sleep eyes, all original in box, circa 1954, $75.00. *Courtesy Kathy & Roy Smith.*

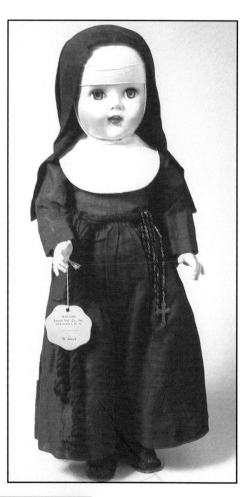

19" hard plastic Madame Louise Doll Co. St. Joseph Nun doll, sleep eyes, open mouth, two upper teeth, no marks on doll, marked hang tag, original black habit in lightweight fabric, wool rope with rosary, circa 1950s, $225.00. *Courtesy Ursula Mertz.*

16" unmarked hard plastic Bride with mohair wig, sleep eyes, lovely color, all original in bride costume, circa 1950s, $275.00. *Courtesy Lourdes Perez-Daple.*

26½" hard plastic IMCO child with stuffed vinyl body, saran hair, rayon dress, beautiful color, circa 1950s, $100.00. *Courtesy Vickie Fronk.*

24" hard plastic Advance Doll & Toy Winnie, the unaided walking talking doll, all original with box, four disks, circa 1954, $200.00. *Courtesy Jeanie Hogh.*

23" Italian hard plastic, flirty eyes, brown mohair wig, cardboard torso, rosy cheeks, original dress, circa 1950s, $250.00. *Courtesy Jean Thompson.*

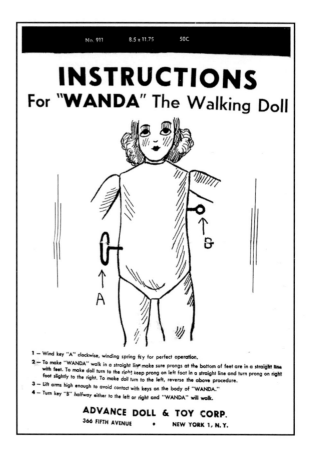

18½" hard plastic Advance Doll & Toy Corp. Wanda, The Walking Doll, sleep eyes, original yellow dress and hat, lovely color, key wound, roller mechanism in white shoes, original box marked *Wanda//Walking//Doll,* circa 1949 – 1955, $200.00. *Courtesy Marie Emmerson.*

Hasbro

G.I. Joe

One of the developments in the doll field has been the action figure, which has produced a whole group of doll collectors who prefer this type of doll. The most famous of those figures has to be G.I. Joe.

G.I. Joe, 1964 – 1976, 11½" tall
Super Joes, 1976 – 1978, 8½" tall
G.I. Joe, 1982 – on, 3½" tall

Jem

Jem dolls were produced by Hasbro in 1985 and 1986. They were patterned after characters in the Jem cartoon series which aired from 1985 to 1988, and was later available as reruns. The complete line of Jem dolls consists of only 21 dolls, but there are a lot of variations and rare fashions to keep the collector hunting. All dolls are 12" tall (except Starlight who is 11"), totally posable as the knees and elbows bend, the waist and head turn, and the wrists swivel. They are realistically proportioned like a human figure. They are made of vinyl with rooted hair. They are marked on head *Hasbro, Inc.* Some backs are marked *COPYRIGHT 1985 HASBRO, INC.//CHINA* and some are marked *COPYRIGHT 1987 HASBRO//MADE IN HONG KONG.* Starlight girls are unmarked. The exciting thing about Jem dolls and the appeal to the public may have been the "truly outrageous" flashy mod fashions and startling hair colors that made them so different from other fashion-type dolls of this era.

12" vinyl Jem wearing On Stage Fashion, There's A Melody Playing, mint-in-package, circa 1985 – 1986, Jem as dressed $185.00; fashion alone in package, $150.00.
Courtesy Linda Holton.

Hitty

Hitty is a character in the book, *Hitty, Her First Hundred Years,* by Rachel Field, published in 1929. It is a story of a 6" doll, Hitty, and her adventures through 100 years. The story remains popular with people who read it as children and give the book to their children and grandchildren. It is charmingly illustrated with pen and ink drawings and early editions also contain some color plates. The original Hitty makes her home in the library in Sturbridge, Massachusetts, while today's artists re-create Hitty for collectors. A Hitty newsletter is published and Hitty get-togethers happen at doll conventions and conferences. See Collectors' Network for information on the Hitty newsletter to keep abreast of latest artist creations.

What to look for:

Re-read the Hitty book to fix in your mind your ideal Hitty and then look for the many artists' interpretations available today. You can find them nude or dressed giving you options on price and the opportunity to make a wardrobe for your own Hitty. You may wish to try carving your own.

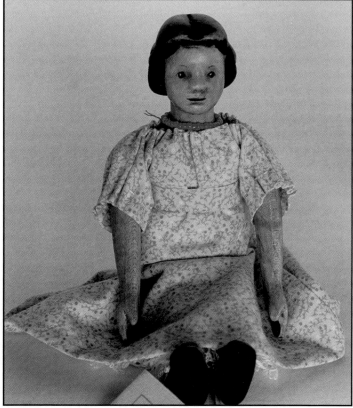

6" wooden jointed Hitty, antiqued to look like original, hand carved by Janci doll artists Nancy Elliot and Jill Sanders, circa 1997, $300.00. *Private collection.*

6" wood Hitty by doll artist Ruth Brown, circa 1997, $200.00.

6" wooden jointed Hitty, hand carved by doll artist Ruth Brown, circa 1997, $200.00.

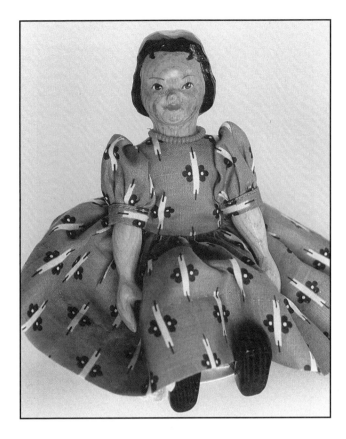

6" wooden jointed Hitty, hand carved by doll artist Patti Hale, circa 1996, $300.00.

6" wooden jointed Hitty in Quaker costume, hand carved by Janci doll artists Nancy Elliot and Jill Sanders, circa 1997, $350.00.

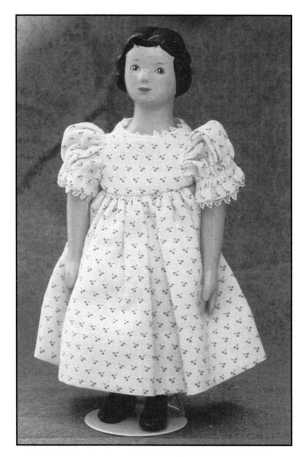

6" wooden jointed Hitty in print dress,
hand carved by Janci doll artists Nancy
Elliot and Jill Sanders, circa 1997, $300.00.

Left: 6" artist doll Hitty basswood with clear tung oil
finish, $350.00; Right: white ash, $400.00; soft
expression, slip, pantaloons, chemise, real coral
beads all hand carved by doll artist Jean Lotz, signed
and dated, circa 1998.

Horsman

Horsman was founded by Edward Imeson Horsman in New York City. It operated from 1865 to 1980+. The E.I. Horsman company distributed, assembled, and made dolls. It merged with Aetna Doll and Toy Co. In 1909 Horsman obtained his first copyright for a complete doll, Billiken. The company later made hard plastic and vinyl dolls many of which are unmarked, some have only a number, and some may be marked *Horsman*. Judds report painted inset pins on the walking mechanism is one means of identification of hard plastic dolls. Some of the hard plastic dolls included Cindy with either a child or fashion-type body.

What to look for:

Composition dolls should have minimal crazing, rosy cheeks, original clothing, labels, or tags when possible. Great characters like the Campbell Kids are always charming. Modern dolls should be perfect and all original. A nifty collecting niche; collectors may find bargains as later Horsman dolls have not been as popular with collectors.

Composition

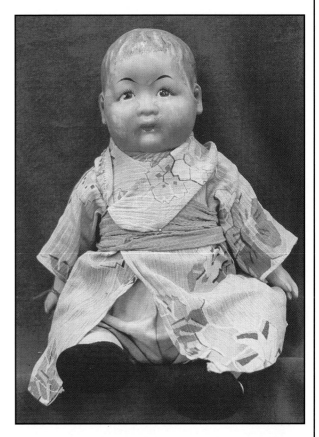

13½" composition Baby Butterfly with painted features, original tagged clothing *Baby Butterfly//Horsman Co. New York//Produced Dec.12, 1913,* some crazing, circa 1913, $650.00. *Courtesy Nelda Shelton.*

12" composition Campbell Kid, five-piece composition body, painted socks and shoes, original clothing, circa 1930 – 1940s, $250.00. *Courtesy McMasters Doll Auctions.*

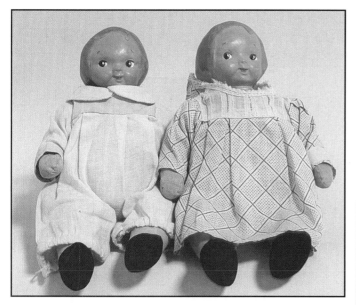

9½" composition Campbell Kids, with straw stuffed
bodies and limbs, mitt hands, original clothes, circa
1910 – 1920, $500.00 for pair.
Courtesy Sue Kinkade.

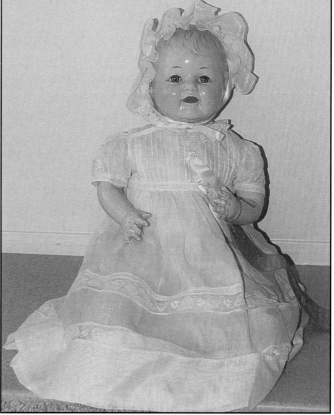

20½" composition Dimples, tin sleep eyes, open
mouth, painted molded hair, circa 1927+, $250.00.
Private collection.

13" composition girl, in blue and pink
Swiss dotted dress and matching bonnet,
mohair wig in pigtails, circa 1938, $200.00.
Courtesy Bev Mitchell.

17" composition boy with sleep eyes, mohair wig, cloth body, composition limbs, tagged *Horsman,* original velvet outfit, overall light crazing, circa 1920s+, $250.00.
Courtesy Debbie Crume.

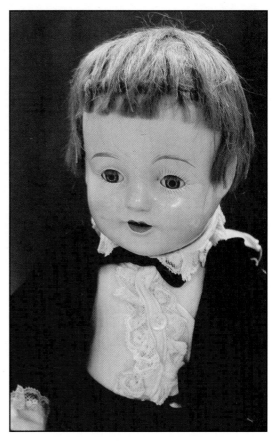

17½" composition Rosebud, cloth body, sleep eyes, original human hair wig, original print dress, circa 1930s, $275.00.
Courtesy Chantal Jeschien.

Vinyl

14" vinyl Baby Precious, boxed, all original, circa 1960s – 1970s, $65.00.
Courtesy McMasters Doll Auctions.

13" vinyl black Baby Bye-Lo drink and wet, mint-in-box, circa 1980, $20.00. *Private collection.*

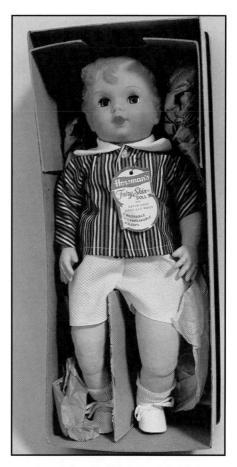

16" early vinyl boy with "fairy skin," an early unstable magic skin type plastic, all original, mint-in-box, circa late 1940s, $125.00. *Courtesy Chantal Jeschien.*

12" and 18" all-vinyl Poor Pitiful Pearl dolls, rooted saran hair, original costume, played with, circa 1959 – 1963, $85.00 and $95.00. *Courtesy Carol Bennett.*

Mary Hoyer

Mary Sensenig Hoyer was born the youngest of 14 children, on October 21, 1901, in Lancaster County, Pennsylvania, to Sallie Whitman and Daniel Sensenig. Her father had a general store and post office in Lancaster, but moved when Mary was six months of age to Mohnton, Pennsylvania, where he again had a store. When she was seven years old the family moved to Reading, Pennsylvania, and she has lived in this area ever since. Her oldest sister, Alice, who did piece work and made cotton sunbonnets with brims of real straw, influenced her.

At age eight, Mary had to be in the hospital with appendicitis, and Alice told her to hurry and get well, because she would buy her a beautiful doll. When she left the hospital, she went home to older sister Alice's house and the doll was waiting for her. Mary remembers the doll being the most beautiful she had ever seen. It had a bisque head with long golden finger curls of human hair, blue eyes, and a smiling mouth with little teeth. The doll was made in Germany and had a jointed body and wore a dress Alice had made for her of blue China silk.

While she was recovering, Alice taught Mary how to knit and crochet and even some simple sewing. Alice eventually opened a store selling yarn, needles, and other related items. Mary, at age 18 attended McCanns Business School, worked for Alice, and began designing and writing knitting instructions.

Mary met William Hoyer in 1923 and they were married in 1926, driving to Canada in a Model T. The honeymooners lived in an apartment until they could build a house nearby in Springmont. Daughter Arlene was born there.

Mary's career began as a designer of knitted and crochetted fashions for children and babies. It seemed a natural outgrowth of that to extend her talents to designing fashions for children's dolls. She first made clothes for her daughter's doll, a 14" heavy composition of unknown maker. Mary soon began dreaming about having an artist make a doll to her own specifications, maybe 14" tall and shaped like a little girl. She first used 13" dolls from Ideal Novelty and Toy Company. Her idea was to sell the nude doll with an accompanying instruction booklet with patterns to knit or crochet outfits for the doll.

About 2,000 of these unmarked Ideal 13" jointed composition dolls were sold before this model was discontinued by Ideal. They had sleep eyes and mohair wigs that came in three different shades; blonde, dark brown, and auburn. The composition bodies had a segmented torso joint just below the arms. The doll sold for $1.50 or you could buy it dressed for $3.00.

In late 1937 Mary met with doll sculptor Bernard Lipfert who had already designed Patsy, Shirley Temple, the Dionne Quintuplets, Ginny, and many other dolls. She told me he did not want to sculpt the doll, but after some conversation and a glass of wine, they came to an agreement. The Fiberoid Doll Company in New York produced the Mary Hoyer doll, but Hoyer retained ownership of the molds. Hoyer estimates approximately 6,500 of the composition dolls were made before the production was discontinued in 1946. Hoyer later discovered that the molds were sold without her knowledge to someone in South America.

Mary Hoyer dolls were unmarked, had painted eyes, and mohair wigs in four shades. The next 5,000 dolls were incised with the mark *THE//MARY HOYER//DOLL.* As soon as sleep eyes were available for composition dolls, they were used, but at first painted eyes were used.

Mary Hoyer

With World War II hard plastic became a popular material for use in dolls. It was new; it was different; it was *modern!* And it appealed to mothers and children. Hoyer began using this material on the new Mary Hoyer dolls. They were also 14" tall, and first had a walking mechanism. This doll was marked in a circle on the back, *ORIGINAL//MARY HOYER//DOLL.* The walker type of body proved troublesome and was removed leaving those models with two slits in the head.

A variation was introduced in 1950, an 18" Mary Hoyer named Gigi. It has the same hard plastic mark as the 14" dolls. Only about 2,000 of these dolls were made by the Frisch Doll Company and they never gained the popularity of the 14" dolls.

Another variant made in the mid-1950s by Ideal had a vinyl head, rooted hair in a ponytail, and high-heeled feet. This doll was discontinued after only one shipment was made. She originally sold for $6.95.

Mary placed ads in *McCall's Needlework and Crafts* magazine and by 1945, Mr. Hoyer quit his job as purchasing agent for Berkshire Knitting Mills to spend full time managing the mail order business, opening a plant and shipping department. Mary also had a retail shop on Penn Street in Reading and another on the Boardwalk in Ocean City, New Jersey, where granddaughter Mary Lynne Sanders remembers playing under the boardwalk in the summer as a little girl.

Another variation was the all-vinyl Vicky doll made in 1957 for Hoyer by Ideal. She came in three sizes, 10½", 12", and 14". The two larger sizes were discontinued and only the 10½" was continued for any length of time. She was described as having a body that bent at the waist, sleep eyes, rooted saran hair, and high-heeled feet. She came dressed in a bra, panties, high heels, and earrings.

The next year, 1958, the Unique Doll Company made Margie, an all-vinyl 10" toddler with rooted hair and sleep eyes, for Hoyer. In 1961 they added a 10" Cathy, an all-vinyl infant made by the same company. Next came an 8" vinyl baby, Janie. Hoyer continued her main marketing thrust with knitted and crocheted patterns, kits, and dressed dolls as well as her custom-made costumes that were sold mail order and retail. The labels read *Mary Hoyer//Reading//PA.*

In 1960, the Fiberoid Doll Company folded after producing approximately 72,000 of the 14" hard plastic dolls, Mary Hoyer's personal favorite. Hoyers next had the 14" doll copied in vinyl, with rooted hair and some face changes. She was called Becky. Becky had long straight, curly, or upswept hairstyles. The hair could be combed, washed, and set, and came in four shades. The Becky doll was unmarked and was discontinued in 1968.

Granddaughter Mary Lynne Saunders continued the Mary Hoyer Doll Company in the 1980s with a vinyl play doll and characters from *The Doll with the Magic Wand,* a fairy tale written by Mary Hoyer. Her 1990s dolls are now more of a basic play doll with a variety of eye colors, hairstyles, and wardrobe. Some of the more intriguing wardrobe available includes hiking boots, shorts, camping gear, and realistic accessories for the modern girls of today. The dolls, clothing, and accessories are forever popular.

Mary Hoyer was a delightful, talented lady, who turned her designing talents into a wonderful career. Her designs, dolls, and patterns will carry on for generations. The Mary Hoyer Doll Company and mail order business is still thriving: Mary Hoyer Doll Company, PO Box 1608, Lancaster, PA 17603, (717) 393-4121.

What to look for:

One of the hottest collectible dolls this past year has been the 18" hard plastic Gigi with the round Mary Hoyer mark on her back. The prices are high for those with original clothing in excellent condition. Mary Hoyer dolls are a great delight for knitters as they get to use all those patterns that have been reissued and are still on the market. Mary Hoyer dolls are a great collectible to look for in composition and hard plastic, but do not pass up the new ones. Look for rosy cheeks, little crazing if composition, clean hard plastic, and original outfits.

16" composition girl in fancy
old, possibly original outfit,
mohair wig, sleep eyes, circa
1940, $375.00.
Courtesy Frances Fabian.

14" hard plastic, with trunk, six outfits, skis, poles,
accessories, and booklets, circa 1940s, $800.00+.
Courtesy Debbie Crume.

14" hard plastic, marked in circle
Mary Hoyer//Original//Doll, nicely re-
dressed in brides dress and veil, circa
1950s, $425.00. *Courtesy Millie Carol.*

Mary Hoyer

14" hard plastic walker with red synthetic wig, beautiful cheek color, redressed, circa mid to late 1940s, $200.00.
Courtesy Joanne Morgan.

14" Perfect on the Ice vinyl play doll, circa 1997, retails for $59.95.
Courtesy Mary Lynne Saunders.

14" Camping vinyl play dolls, circa 1997, retails for $59.95.
Courtesy Mary Lynne Saunders.

Ideal

Ideal Novelty and Toy Co. (1906 – 1990+, Brooklyn, NY) produced their own composition dolls in the early years. Morris Michtom started the business making teddy bears in 1906 with his wife, Rose. Michtom also began making composition "unbreakable" dolls about this time. His early comic characters were popular. Ideal also produced licensed dolls for companies to help promote their products such as Uneeda Kid that carried a small box of crackers for the Uneeda Biscuit Company. Some of their big successes were Shirley Temple in composition, Saucy Walker and Toni in hard plastic, and Miss Revlon in vinyl. They also made dolls of cloth and rubber. They used various marks including *IDEAL* (in a diamond) *US of A; IDEAL Novelty and Toy Co., Brooklyn, New York,* and others.

What to look for:

Look for dolls with minimal crazing in composition, good color, and original clothing. Hard plastic and vinyl dolls should have very good color, and clean, bright, perhaps tagged original clothing. A wide variety of Ideal dolls are available as they were in business for so many years.

Composition

14" composition Tickletoes with flange neck, flirty eyes, open mouth for pacifier, cloth body, rubber arms and legs, original outfit with tag, paint flaking, circa 1928 – 1939, $200.00. *Private collection.*

12" composition Flexy Fanny Bryce as Baby Snooks, wood torso and feet, flexible wire arms and legs, designed by Joseph Kallus, painted features, molded hair with loop, original costume, circa 1938, $295.00. *Courtesy Odis Gregg.*

13" composition Flexy Sunny Sam, painted molded hair, flexible wire arms and legs, wooden torso and feet, felt suspenders, pants with patches, circa 1938+, $185.00.
Courtesy Iva Mae Jones.

21" composition Deanna Durbin unplayed-with condition, circa 1938 – 1941, $1,700.00.
Courtesy McMasters Doll Auctions.

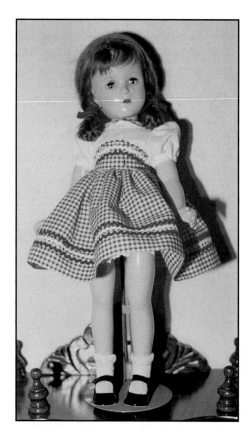

18" composition Margaret O'Brien, child movie star, nicely re-dressed, circa 1946, $600.00.
Courtesy Diane Graves.

Hard Plastic and Vinyl Baby

7" vinyl black Baby Baby a Handful of Love, one-piece vinyl body, black rooted hair, turn bottle and her eyes close, circa 1976 – 1977, $35.00.
Courtesy Cathie Clark.

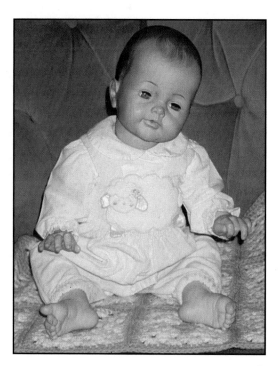

25" all-vinyl Bye-Bye Baby, fully jointed, painted molded brown hair, re-dressed, circa 1960 – 1961, $225.00.
Courtesy Barb Hilliker.

14" vinyl Moon Beam baby character from Dick Tracy comic strip, daughter of Junior Tracy and Moon Maid, cloth body, painted eyes, missing clear plastic space helmet, crier, circa 1965, $35.00. *Courtesy Shirley Eshom.*

20" vinyl Snoozie, all original in box, blonde rooted saran hair, sleep eyes, turn knob she squirms, opens and closes her eyes and cries, cloth body with vinyl arms and legs, circa 1964, $55.00. *Courtesy Iva Mae Jones.*

18" vinyl Thumbelina cloth body, all original with tag, circa 1983 – 1985, $45.00. *Courtesy Marie Rodgers.*

Hard Plastic and Vinyl, Child or Adult

13½" vinyl Cinnamon, originally called Velvet's Little Sister, painted eyes, rooted auburn growing hair, orange polka dot outfit, also has other outfits available, circa 1972 – 1974, $40.00. *Courtesy Penny Pittsley.*

18" vinyl Crissy with vinyl body, swivel waist, growing hair, original turquoise outfit, with box, circa 1969, $50.00.
Courtesy Angie Gonzales.

22" vinylite Judy Splinters, open/closed mouth with molded tongue, painted eyes, yarn like pigtails, character from TV show, rewigged, re-dressed, circa 1950, $75.00. *Courtesy Janet Hill.*

Ideal

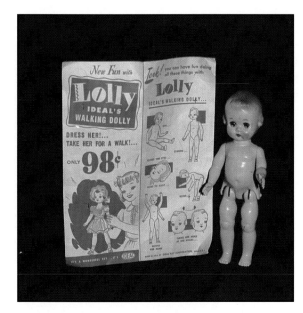

9½" hard plastic Lolly, also known as Tiny Girl, all hard plastic, jointed arms, head turns and she walks, circa 1951 – 1955, $30.00. *Courtesy Cathie Clark.*

16" hard plastic Mary Hartline in rare green dress, circa 1952, $450.00. *Courtesy Iva Mae Jones.*

16" hard plastic Mary Hartline, fully jointed, blue sleep eyes with black eyeshadow over and under eyes, Mary Hartline was an ABC-TV star on Super Circus, circa 1952, $350.00. *Courtesy Cathie Clark.*

14" hard plastic Miss Curity,
saran wig, sleep eyes with black
eyeshadow, has a Bauer and
Black Curity first aid kit, uses
Toni P 90 body, circa 1954,
$325.00. *Courtesy Cathie Clark.*

20" vinyl Miss Revlon tagged, boxed, all original,
marked *VT-20* on back of head, fashion-type body,
high heeled, with saran wig, circa 1956 – 1959,
$650.00. *Courtesy McMasters Doll Auctions.*

20" vinyl Miss Revlon in Cherries a la
Mode red and white dress, circa 1956+,
$250.00. *Courtesy June Algeier.*

17" vinyl Miss Revlon, rooted hair, sleep eyes, circa 1958 – 1959, $175.00.
Courtesy Cathie Clark.

15" vinyl Miss Revlon, swivel waist, blue sleep eyes, earrings, circa 1958 – 1959, $125.00.
Courtesy Cathie Clark.

10½" all-vinyl Little Miss Revlon, fully jointed, high-heeled feet, swivel waist, rooted hair, sleep eyes, pierced ears, circa 1958, $100.00.
Courtesy Cathie Clark.

10½" all-vinyl Little Miss Revlon, fully jointed, high-heeled feet, swivel waist, rooted hair, sleep eyes, pierced ears, circa 1958 – 1960, $145.00.
Courtesy Cathie Clark.

10½" vinyl Little Miss Revlon, swivel waist, high-heeled feet, rooted hair, sleep eyes, pierced ears, all original, with rosy cheeks, circa 1958 – 1960, $125.00. *Courtesy Chantal Jeschien.*

10½" vinyl Little Miss Revlon and her bridal gown in their original marked boxes, circa 1958 – 1960, $195.00. *Courtesy McMasters Doll Auctions.*

36" vinyl Patty Playpal, jointed wrists, sleep eyes, rooted saran wig, closed mouth, bright cheek color, circa 1959, $200.00. *Courtesy Kathy & Roy Smith.*

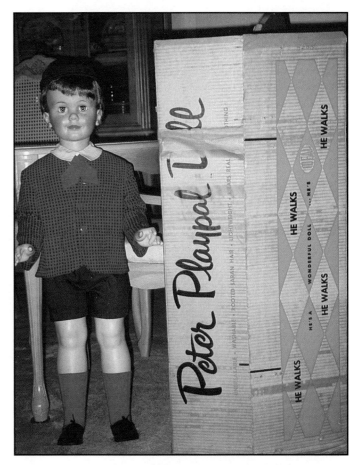

38" vinyl Peter Playpal with red jacket, black pants, with box, circa 1960 – 1961, $800.00. *Courtesy Iva Mae Jones.*

15" all hard plastic Sara Ann, saran wig, sleep eyes, fully jointed, uses the Toni body, but the company did not have to pay royalties to the Toni company, circa 1951, $175.00. *Courtesy Cathie Clark.*

14" all hard plastic Toni, mint in her original box, fully jointed, sleep eyes, platinum wig, came with hair wave kit, marked *P-90,* circa 1949 – 1953, $500.00. *Courtesy Cathie Clark.*

14" hard plastic Toni, fully jointed with sleep eyes, Dupont nylon glued-on wig, came with kit containing curlers and playwave solution of sugar water, circa 1949 – 1953, $500.00. *Courtesy Cathie Clark.*

22½" all hard plastic Toni, fully jointed, sleep eyes, glued-on platinum wig, marked *P-94,* circa 1949 – 1953, $700.00. *Courtesy Cathie Clark.*

14" hard plastic Toni, fully jointed, sleep eyes, red nylon wig, marked *P-90,* circa 1949 – 1953, $500.00.
Courtesy Cathie Clark.

16" hard plastic Toni, fully jointed, sleep eyes, blonde nylon wig, marked *P 91,* circa 1949 – 1953, $550.00.
Courtesy Cathie Clark.

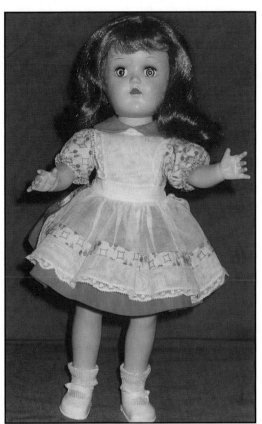

16" hard plastic Toni, fully jointed, sleep eyes, blonde nylon wig, marked *P-91*, circa 1949 – 1953, $300.00. *Courtesy Cathie Clark.*

14" hard plastic Toni, original tagged dress, circa 1949+, $225.00. *Courtesy Micki Beston.*

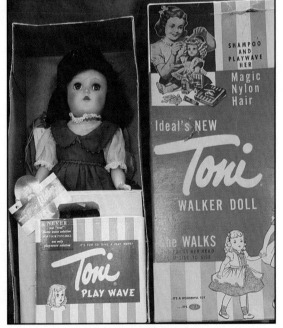

14" hard plastic Toni, marked *P-90,* mint in box, unusual with brown eyes, beautiful color, original outfit, play wave accessories, circa 1949, $600.00+. *Courtesy Rae Klenke.*

Kenner

The *Star Wars* movie was made in 1977, and the sequel, *The Empire Strikes Back,* in 1980. Kenner made Star Wars figures in 1978 in Hong Kong, ranging in height from 7" to 15". They included Princess Leia Organa, Luke Sykwalker, R2-D2, Chewbaca, Darth Vader, and C-3P0. In 1979 Boba Fett, Han Solo, Stormtrooper, Ben (Obi-Wan) Kenobi, Jawa, and IG-88 were added. They also made small 3 – 4" figures starting in 1979.

What to look for:

Kenner has made a variety of modern character dolls such as Bob Scout with Boy Scout uniform and accessories, and sports figures and fashion-type dolls. Look for clean all original dolls with good color. Star Wars figures are more popular with toy collectors, but are always collectible, as are celebrities such as Six Million Dollar Man figures. Look for them at garage sales, flea markets, and estate sales.

12½" vinyl Darci, auburn rooted hair, long turquoise gown, on plastic stand, jointed hands, posable elbows and knees, circa 1978, $45.00. *Private collection.*

13" vinyl Jaime Sommers Bionic Woman, all original in box, blonde rooted hair, painted features, open mouth with teeth, circa 1976, $75.00. *Courtesy Penny Pittsley.*

Klumpe

Klumpe made caricature figures of felt over wire armature with painted mask faces in Barcelona, Spain, from 1952 to the mid-1970s. Figures represent professionals, hobbyists, Spanish dancers, historical characters, and contemporary males and females performing a wide variety of tasks. Of the 200 or more different figures, the most common are Spanish dancers, bull fighters, and doctors. Some Klumpes were imported by Effanbee in the early 1950s. Originally the figures had two sewn-on identifying cardboard tags.

What to look for:

These amusing characters may be missing their tags, but are still very collectible. Often passed over by more sophisticated collectors, they can still be found for reasonable prices. Look for those with more accessories, tags, or labels. They should be clean with bright colors. The more intricate the costume and accessories, the more desirable they are to collectors. They must be pristine with all labels to command highest prices. Keep on the lookout at estate sales, antique malls, flea markets, and doll shows for these.

11" felt bellhop carrying suitcase, birdcage, hatbox, and other accessories, very good condition, gold foil label, white paper tag, circa 1952 – 1975, $70.00.
Courtesy Carol Bennett.

10½" cloth unmarked Klumpe-type cowboy, circa 1950s – 1960s, $78.00.
Courtesy Christine McWilliams.

10" cloth fisherman with pole, fish, and newspaper, circa 1960s, $150.00. *Courtesy Sharon Kolibaba.*

11" cloth Spanish dancer with painted features, all original, tag attached to skirt, circa 1952 – 1970s, $125.00.
Courtesy Sharon Kolibaba.

Lawton

Wendy Lawton was born in San Francisco, and attended and graduated from California schools. There, she met and married her husband, Keith, and made her home in Turlock, California, with their two children Rebecca and Patrick. Her interests have developed around her home and her own artistic achievements. She was guided early on by doll maker Thelma Hanke who taught her all phases of doll making including making wigs, costuming, and fabrics.

Wendy is an avid reader and has been inspired by children's literature and classics to bring to life her own dolls. The family company has greatly expanded, but is still overseen by Wendy who designs, sculpts, and paints all prototypes, designs their costumes, and does some painting on the final dolls. Wendy enjoys the challenge of researching each new subject by reading and conceptualizing the character before designing the doll. Lawton's Josephine, the souvenir doll for the UFDC Region 2 North Conference in Modesto was a big hit, and quickly more than doubled the registration fee in price. The companion piece was a suitcase with extra garments, exquisitely made, as are all of the special accessories that accompany Lawton dolls.

Lawton has been a DOTY Award nominee many times and her dolls are eagerly sought after for special souvenirs. See Collectors' Network for information on the Lawton Collectors' Guild.

What to look for:

The great workmanship on Lawton dolls with wonderful wardrobe and accessories make this very modern doll a collectible that seems sure to increase in value. You may wish to add them to your collection just because you like them. These porcelain dolls sometimes turn up at doll shows still at reasonable prices. They are generally not large dolls, often under 14" tall.

9" porcelain Beatrice Louise made for the UFDC New Orleans Adventures on the Orient Express Luncheon, limited to 310, wooden body, with companion suitcase, wardrobe, circa 1998, $600.00+. *Private collection.*

13" all-porcelain Bessie and her Bye-Lo, a limited edition, circa 1990s, $595.00.
Courtesy Millie Carol.

14" porcelain Katie and her Kewpie, 1994 collection, boxed, limited edition of 750, circa 1994, $595.00.
Courtesy Iva Mae Jones.

13" porcelain Little Colonel, boxed, limited to 250 dolls with numbered certificates of authenticity, signed by Wendy Lawton, circa 1990, $500.00.
Courtesy Iva Mae Jones.

14" porcelain Pascha, named after the Russian word for Easter, carrying an exquisitely painted Pysanky egg, authentically dressed in heavily hand-embroidered Ukrainian costume, limited 750, circa 1992, $495.00.
Courtesy Iva Mae Jones.

13" porcelain Patricia and her Patsy (6½"), limited edition, signed *Wendy Lawton* on back of head, circa 1995, $595.00.
Courtesy Millie Carol.

Lenci

Elena von Konig Scavini was born in Italy in 1886, and after the loss of her firstborn child, she started making cuddly dolls. She called the dolls Lencina or Little Lenci. Her dolls were used as decorative accessories in bedrooms and cars and were carried with designer costumes. Early dolls were characters, tagged with small Lenci button. Many, and some of the most intricate, were made during the 1920s. This era is noted for rooted hair, hand embroidery, and pieced felt costumes with felt flowers. The American stock market crash threw the company into bankruptcy. It was taken over by Pilade Garella who narrowed the product line from clothing, costumes, ceramics, furniture, and handbags to only dolls. The 1930s dolls were simpler and there were fewer styles. Mascottes (7½") and miniature (9") dolls in regional, nursery rhyme, and children's clothing were heavily produced and promoted. Glass flirty eyes were added in 1935. Baby dolls were introduced in the 1930s with two face models, but they were not popular. Boudoir dolls, with elongated arms and legs dressed as celebrities, were very popular and made throughout the company's history. By 1940, Madame Lenci had lost her husband, Enrico, sold her remaining shares in the Lenci Company, and severed all ties to it. In the 1940s, Lenci quality diminished. In 1942, Beppe Garella, Pilade's son came into the business. He became president after his father's death in 1968. In the 1950s, the Lenci dolls' popularity again slowed and the company made dolls of other materials. In 1978, the company again started making felt dolls and this move was profitable. Madame Lenci died in 1974, and in 1993, Beppe Garella died. His daughter Bibija now runs the company.

What to look for:

It is important to remember that Lenci dolls are made of felt. Some identification tips include ears made with double layers of material, and dolls may wear scalloped cotton socks. Felt costumes and extra accessories were found with dolls of the 1920s and 1930s. Dolls made in the 1920s can have rooted mohair wigs. Wigs from the 1930s may be frizzy from play. Dolls made in the 1940s may have hard cardboard-type felt faces. Look for dolls that are clean with bright colors, accessories, and original costumes.

16" felt Baby, with 159 style face, all original in pink costume, circa 1930s, $1,700.00.
Courtesy Nancy Lazenby.

Lenci

7½" felt twins, all original (twins look at one another), shown with felt dogs not original to pair but a great accessory, circa 1930s, $1,200.00 for pair; dogs, $125.00 each.
Courtesy Nancy Lazenby.

9½" felt girl, perhaps the low version of a line of more expensive dolls pictured in 1923 *Playthings* ad, pinked edge on red skirt, few applied flowers, metal button reads *LENCI* on underwear, circa 1923, $800.00. *Courtesy Nancy Lazenby.*

9" felt flapper girl, painted features, side-glancing eyes, original costume, lacks hatbox, circa 1920s, $400.00.
Courtesy Nancy Lazenby.

9" felt Pan, half boy, half goat creature called a fetish, considered a good luck charm, loop on head to hang up, mohair lower legs, wooden hooves, carries wooden flute, circa 1920s, $1,200.00. *Courtesy Nancy Lazenby.*

9" felt Annie Ronnie miniature, mint condition, circa 1930s, $450.00. *Courtesy Nancy Lazenby.*

12" felt smoking boy, hard cardboard-like face, cotton clothing, unusual because he is a child smoking, circa 1940s, $500.00. *Courtesy Nancy Lazenby.*

14" felt Jr. Fascist boy, all original with pin in hat, circa 1930s, $1,500.00. *Courtesy Nancy Lazenby.*

Lenci

14½" cloth mountain climber smoker with cigarette in mouth, painted side-glancing brown eyes, hang tag, all original, with walking stick, circa 1920s, $895.00. *Courtesy Bette Yadon.*

17½" felt boy with painted side-glancing eyes, mohair wig, original clothes, some wear, circa 1920s, $425.00. *Courtesy Suzanne Fetsco.*

13" felt Series III, all original, mohair wig in original set, circa 1930s, $1,200.00, Steiff accessory chicken not original to doll, $125.00. *Courtesy Nancy Lazenby.*

Left: 17" felt 300 Series doll,
circa 1930s, $2,250.00;
Right: 20½" felt Lenci, has same
face, but now model BH with
costume number, circa 1940s,
$1,500.00. *Courtesy Nancy Lazenby.*

16" cloth girl, marked *Sarda* on paper
tag on hand, and *Modello Depositato,
Torino, Made in Italy,* painted brown
eyes, original felt costume, circa 1930s,
$525.00. *Courtesy McMasters Doll Auctions.*

13" felt Series 111 girl in yellow
organdy, all original, near mint, hair
in original set, circa 1930s, $1,200.00.
Courtesy Nancy Lazenby.

Lenci

17½" felt Tyrolean girl, 300 Series, shows intricate costuming company is famous for, pierced earrings are rare, circa 1929, $2,000.00.
Courtesy Nancy Lazenby.

18" felt girl, original pink, blue, and white organdy costume, hollow torso, hair sewn on concentric circles of wefting, circa late 1930s or early 1940s, $1,300.00.
Courtesy Nancy Lazenby.

16" felt Dutch pair (when packaged as a pair, will always look at one another), Dutch boy has original pipe in drilled hole in mouth, girl carries goose, $50.00, not original to doll, circa 1930s, $2,000.00 pair.
Courtesy Nancy Lazenby.

23" felt girl in Southern belle type red taffeta costume, organdy bonnet, with handmade flowers on crown, this face only used after 1940, mint in box, $2,300.00.
Courtesy Nancy Lazenby.

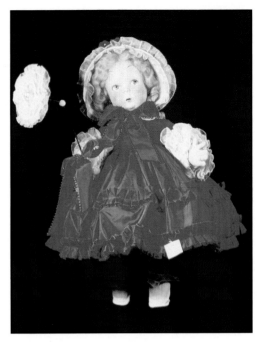

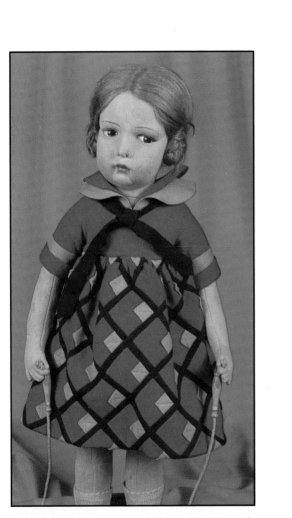

22" felt child, pressed felt swivel head, painted brown eyes, closed mouth, mohair wig in coiled braids, holding her original jump rope, cloth torso with felt arms and legs, circa 1920s – 1930s, $575.00.
Courtesy McMasters Doll Auctions.

18" wool felt Diana doll, *N0963301* on wrist tag, hand painted gold and silver pin, Princess Diana was presented with the gift of a beautiful doll named after her during a trip to Italy in 1985, circa 1985, $195.00.
Courtesy Iva Mae Jones.

Lenci

18½" felt girl, oil painted pressed mask face, applied ears, brown painted eyes, felt arms and legs, cloth body, blonde mohair wig, blue dotted ray dress with felt trim, blue felt bow, blue felt shoes, circa 1940s, $600.00. *Courtesy Dee Cermak.*

10" felt Lenci-type crow, made by E.B.I. Florence Italy, circa 1950s, $200.00. *Courtesy Nancy Lazenby.*

15" total length, cloth clown hand puppet with winking eye, very rare, circa 1920s – 1930s, $225.00. *Courtesy Nancy Lazenby.*

Company made many accessories such as baskets, purses, crowns of flowers, sewing kits, lapel pins, and perfume bottles. Accessories were more abundant in 1920s – 1930s. Perfume or pin in original box, $75.00 each. *Courtesy Nancy Lazenby.*

13" cloth girl, original outfit, some wear, $400.00. *Courtesy Connie Baca.*

11" felt Eros doll, a Lenci-type, very expressive painted eyes, all original, circa 1930s – 1940s, $225.00. *Courtesy Nancy Lazenby.*

Lenci

18" felt unmarked Lenci-type girl with painted eyes, pin, aqua felt hat and coat, blonde mohair wig, circa 1920s – 1930s, $200.00. *Courtesy Suzanne Fetsco.*

Two felt Eros Lenci-type girls, 11" in pink, $250.00; and 16" pink and black coat and hat, $400.00; circa 1930s. Eros dolls have silky sock with machine stitched hem across the top, shoes have metal button closure, Lenci's did not. *Courtesy Nancy Lazenby.*

Mattel, Inc.

Mattel was founded in 1945 in Los Angeles, California, and has been a dominant force in the doll industry with their Barbie, Chatty Cathy, and others. The company began when Ruth and Elliott Handler and their friend Harold Mattson founded the Mattel company. The name came from "Matt" for Mattson and "el" for Elliot. They began by first making picture frames, evolving into toy furniture. Mattson left the company because of ill health and Ruth Handler began to handle marketing. She advertised in 1955 on a children's TV show, *The Mickey Mouse Club*. In 1959, they marketed Barbie, named after their daughter, and the company prospered. Barbie (see separate section) has become the number one collectible doll in the world. Mattel also has manufactured quite a list of celebrity dolls as well as characters from TV shows. The Handlers are no longer associated with the company.

What to look for:

These modern vinyl and hard plastic dolls are very collectible because so many kids played with them. Look for those still with boxes and accessories.

Baby

17" vinyl Baby Say 'n' See, eyes and lips move when talking, played with, still talks, circa 1967 – 1968, $35.00. *Private collection.*

17" vinyl Baby Secret, original outfit with name on bib, blue eyes, red rooted hair, stuffed body, played with, circa 1966 – 1967, $35.00. *Private collection.*

Mattel, Inc.

16" vinyl Chatty Patty talker, mint in box, circa 1983, $75.00. *Private collection.*

7" vinyl Cheerful Tearful in original outfit on left, re-dressed on right, circa 1966, $15.00 each. *Courtesy Millie Carol.*

15½" vinyl Drowsy pull string talker, cloth body, rooted hair, painted eyes with molded drooping lids, played with condition, circa 1965 – 1974, $8.00. *Courtesy Marie Rodgers.*

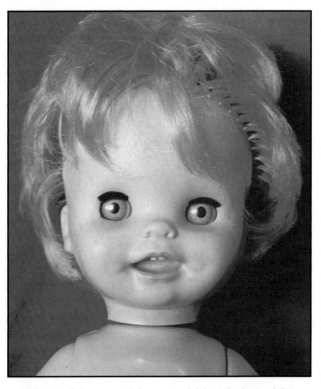

16" vinyl Saucy with rooted blonde hair, blue eyes, when left arm is rotated eyes flirt, face changes expression, circa 1973, nude, $35.00. *Private collection.*

Child

19" vinyl Chatty Cathy, hard plastic body, pull string talker, blue sleep eyes, rooted hair, freckles, open/closed mouth with two teeth, original sundress not complete, does not talk, circa 1962 – 1964, $75.00.
Courtesy Darleen Foote.

20" all-vinyl Chatty Cathy, pull string activates voice, blue party dress, she is standing by her original stroller, circa 1963 – 1965, set $250.00.
Courtesy Cathie Clark.

24" soft vinyl Charmin' Chatty, hard vinyl body, long rooted hair, plays vinyl record through a slot in her side, circa 1963 – 1964 $225.00. *Courtesy Cathie Clark.*

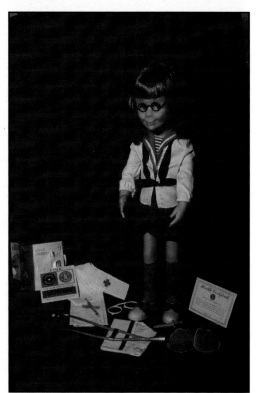

Mattel, Inc.

24" vinyl Charmin' Chatty came with five records to be placed in slot on left side of doll to play, rooted blonde hair, wears extra outfit available for her, no records, does not talk, circa 1963 – 1964, $95.00. *Courtesy Penny Pittsley.*

6½" vinyl Buffy holding Mrs. Beasley with the hard to keep black glasses, tagged, circa 1967+, $150.00.
Courtesy Bonnie Baskins.

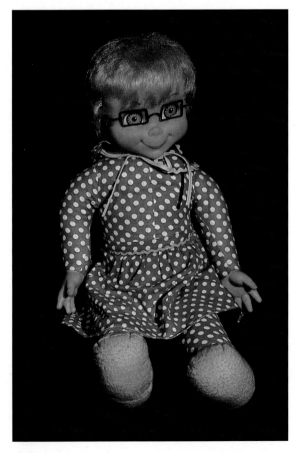

22" vinyl talking Mrs. Beasley from the hit TV show *Family Affair* cloth stuffed body, pull string talking mechanism, square vinyl glasses, circa 1967 – 1974, $225.00. *Courtesy Cathie Clark.*

16" vinyl talking Sister Belle, cloth body, yarn hair, TV character, pull string talker, says 11 different phrases, #0730, circa 1961 – 1963, $175.00.
Courtesy Marie Emmerson.

Adult

18" vinyl Hot Looks with rooted
synthetic hair, decal type eyes, earrings, stockinet body, circa 1986,
played with condition, $12.00.
Courtesy Marie Rodgers.

Mattel, Inc.

11½" vinyl Twist 'n Turn Julia, near mint in box, circa 1969, $165.00. *Courtesy McMasters Doll Auctions.*

11½" all-vinyl Starr, bendable knees, painted features, jointed at wrists, blonde rooted hair, circa 1979, $35.00. *Courtesy Cathie Clark.*

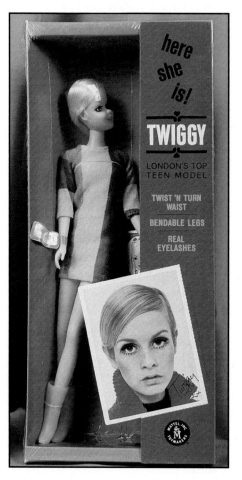

11½" vinyl Twist 'n Turn Twiggy, in box, #1185, near mint in box, circa 1967, $230.00. *Courtesy McMasters Doll Auctions.*

Nancy Ann Storybook

Nancy Ann Storybook Dolls was started in 1936, in San Francisco, California, by Rowena Haskin (Nancy Ann Abbott). The dolls were painted bisque with mohair wigs and painted eyes. Their heads were molded to their torsos, and they had jointed limbs. They either had a sticker on their outfit or a hang tag. They also made a hard plastic 8" Muffie and various sizes of Miss Nancy Ann Style Show, and an 11" Debbie and 7½" Lori Ann with vinyl heads and hard plastic bodies. In the 1950s and 1960s they made 10½" Miss Nancy Ann and Little Miss Nancy Ann, vinyl high-heeled fashion-type dolls.

What to look for:

The newer dolls need to be complete and mint. That is what collectors are looking for. In competition, the older, rare, mint, original, and beautiful doll is the one that catches the judges' eyes. That leaves a lot of played with and soiled dolls with faded clothing or missing accessories that are still collectible, and perhaps you can salvage some great dolls that others have skipped over. You can certainly find enough to collect, but always look for the one with the more intricate costume, prettier coloring, and original clothing, tags, labels, or in boxes.

5" painted bisque Nancy Ann Storybook in white box with blue dots, To Market, To Market #120, silver label, excellent condition, plaid dress, brochure, bracelet, circa 1941 – 1942, $75.00. *Courtesy Arthur Mock.*

5" painted bisque Nancy Ann Storybook in blue box with white dots, jointed legs, painted molded socks and shoes, booklet, missing bracelet, circa 1940, $150.00. *Courtesy Arthur Mock.*

5" painted bisque Nancy Ann Storybook in white box, pink dots, Thursdays Child Has Far to Go #183, silver label brochure, no bracelet, circa 1943 – 1947, $75.00. *Courtesy Arthur Mock.*

5½" painted bisque Nancy Ann Storybook in original costume, painted eyes, brown mohair wig, painted shoes, circa 1940s, $10.00. *Courtesy Millie Carol.*

Two 8" hard plastic Nancy Ann Storybook Muffie dolls, original outfits, circa 1953 – 1956, $345.00 for pair. *Courtesy McMasters Doll Auctions.*

Early Muffie brochure, $25.00.
Courtesy Cathie Clark.

Old Cottage Toys

This firm was founded in 1948 by Mrs. Margaret. E. Fleischmann, who fled to England from her native Czechoslovakia during the war years. Mrs. Fleischmann made dolls for her daughter Suzanne and then for sale. The heads are made of a hard composition/hard plastic type material, with bodies of felt over padded wire armature. The features are molded and painted with mohair wigs. Fleischmann registered her trademark in 1948. The dolls have an oval paper hang tag with a cottage picured on one side and marked *Old Cottage Doll Made in England* on the other. They made historical figures, literary figures, and English policemen, guards, and pearly figures. In 1968 she made Tweedledee and Tweedledum for a B.B.C. production of Lewis Carrol's *Through the Looking-Glass*.

What to look for:

This category of dolls is currently sought after, very collectible, and rising in value. Most desired are the literary characters, pearly dolls, and dolls with added detail. Finding Tweedledee or Tweedledum in a box would be very lucky. Dolls should be clean, tagged, and original to command highest prices.

9½" composition doll with baby, all original, circa 1948+, $200.00.
Courtesy Nancy Lazenby.

10" English composition doll, original costume, circa 1950s, $175.00.
Courtesy Dorothy Bohlin.

Old Cottage Toys

10" English composition matron with baby, original costume, hang tag, circa 1950s, $175.00.
Courtesy Dorothy Bohlin.

8" pair of English composition dolls in Tyrolean costume, hang tag, circa 1950s, $95.00 each.
Courtesy Dorothy Bohlin.

13½" vinyl Ursli #39.83,
painted features, blonde wig,
freckles, cloth body, circa
1983, $250.00.
Courtesy Linda Maddux.

16" vinyl Karli #44.84 with blond wig, brown
eyes, all original in navy blue sweater, short
blue pants, circa 1984, $280.00.
Courtesy Linda Maddux.

18" vinyl Sylvie with cloth body, all
original, circa 1989, $300.00.
Courtesy Millie Busch.

Heidi Ott

19" vinyl Quinta #K5.85, open/closed mouth, brown eyes, human hair wig, all original in print dress with white apron, cloth body, circa 1985, $375.00.
Courtesy Linda Madden.

19" vinyl Serina #2.84, with human hair wig, brown eyes, cloth body, red dress with pinafore, circa 1984, $300.00. *Courtesy Linda Maddux.*

Ronnaug Petterssen

Ronnaug Petterssen (Norway, 1901 – 1980) was an art student in Germany in 1929. She also traveled to Spain and other countries to study folk costumes. She became a member of the Norwegian Association for Arts and Crafts and won prizes for her doll-making abilities. Petterssen created a Norwegian doll exhibit for the 1937 World Exhibition in Paris, in 1939 her dolls were shown in the New York World's Fair, and after World War II they were shown internationally. Known for her attention to detail in costuming, she managed to include essential motifs even in smaller 8" dolls. Petterssen maintained a studio in Oslo, Norway, and utilized cottage industry workers to make costumes from the patterns she designed. The heads of the larger dolls are press molded of felt, while the smaller dolls may be felt or other materials. Dolls are not marked, but all had a blue-gold round dime-sized paper tag attached with gold thread on clothing. One side reads *Ronnaug Petterssen* and the other has a drawing of a Laplander and *Made in Norway//Vare Marke*. Some smaller dolls have also been found of celluloid.

What to look for:

Petterssen dolls are noted for their quality construction, excellent workmanship, and attention to detail. Dolls range in size from 8" to 18", with painted or glass eyes, and may only have gold thread left where tag was attached. Look for those that are clean with bright colors. Again, a "sleeper" in the collectible world because so little is known of them.

9½" painted celluloid girl in original Norwegian regional dress, side-glancing eyes, circa 1950s, $40.00.
Courtesy Joanne Morgan.

Quintuplets

Alexander Doll Co. won the license to produce the official Dionne quintuplet dolls after the girls' birth in 1934 to a Canadian farm couple. Designed by Bernard Lipfert, they were all composition with painted eyes, molded hair, and jointed baby bodies. They were also made as toddlers in different sizes. Not to be outdone, other companies came out with their own sets of five babies to try to capitalize on the buying frenzy. Quint collectors have their own newsletter and collect all sorts of related memorabilia as well as the dolls. See Collectors' Network for information on the *Quint News*.

What to look for:

Dolls should be clean and bright, with good color and original clothing. Look for dolls other than Alexanders, as other companies made dolls to compete with the licensee. Other quints should not be priced as high as Alexanders.

7" composition Madame Alexander Dionne Quintuplets painted brown eyes to side, closed mouths, painted molded hair, composition bent-limb baby bodies, circa 1935 – 1945, $1,125.00.
Courtesy McMasters Doll Auctions.

3" – 4" Quintuplets and
Nurse on round card, nurse
still tied on, $125.00.
Courtesy Connie Lee Martin.

7" vinyl Madame Alexander Fisher
Quint, unmarked, original outfit,
circa 1964 only, $100.00.
Courtesy Millie Carol.

Raggedy Ann & Andy

Raggedy Ann and Andy were designed by Johnny Gruelle in 1915, and made by various companies. Ann wears a dress with an apron, Andy a shirt and pants with matching hat.

P.J. Volland, 1920 – 34

Early dolls marked *Patented Sept. 7, 1915.* All-cloth, tin or wooden button eyes, painted features. Some have sewn knee or arm joints, brown or auburn sparse yarn hair, oversize hands, feet turned outward.

Mollye Goldman, 1935 – 38

Marked on chest: *Raggedy Ann and Andy Dolls Manufactured by Mollye's Doll Outfitters.* Nose outlined in black, red heart on chest, reddish orange hair, multicolored legs, blue feet, some have oil cloth faces.

Georgene Novelties, 1938 – 62

Ann has orange hair and a top knot, six different mouth styles, early dolls had tin eyes, later plastic, six different noses, seams in middle of legs and arms to represent knees and elbows, feet turn forward, red and white striped legs. All have hearts that say *I love you* printed on chest. Tag sewn to left side seam, several variations, all say *Georgene Novelties, Inc.*

Knickerbocker, 1962 – 82

Printed features, hair color changes from orange to red; there were five mouth and five eyelash variations, tags were located on clothing back or pant seam.

What to look for:

Dolls that are clean, no rips or tears, original clothing, tags, or labels. Raggedy Ann was so loved that many are too worn to collect, but they are still available and eagerly sought by collectors.

17½" cloth Volland Raggedy Andy and 16½" Volland Raggedy Ann played with condition, circa 1920 – 1934, $2,000.00 for pair.

15½" cloth Georgene Novelties Raggedy Andy and 15" Raggedy Ann some fading, soil, circa 1930s – 1960s, $375.00 for pair. *Courtesy Debbie Crume.*

19" cloth Georgene Novelties Raggedy Ann, no apron, water stain, circa 1947, $245.00. *Courtesy Debbie Crume.*

18" cloth Georgene Novelties Raggedy Ann, re-dressed, tagged body, wear spot on face, circa 1950s, $95.00. *Courtesy Debbie Crume.*

Richwood

Richwood Toys, Inc., was located in Annapolis, Maryland. Sandra Sue was produced from the late 1940s through the 1950s. The only marks are numbers under her arm or leg. Sandra Sue was a high quality doll, similar to others produced at this time, but with more attributes than most.

Sandra Sue had sleep eyes with molded lashes, closed mouth, jointed arms and legs. She was made as a walker and non-walker, and had an extensive wardrobe available for her as well as a line of furniture. She had saran wigs and a suggestion of a fashion body with gently molded breasts and a slimmer waist. She was modeled with both flat and high-heel feet. One tip for identification is dark orange painted eyebrows and painted lashes below eyes. The hands are formed with fingers together, separate thumbs, and the palms face in to the body. Her head did not turn when she walked.

Sandra Sue's wardrobe would be the envy of many of the contemporary dolls. It included evening and bridal gowns, sports wear such as ski apparel and skating costumes, skirts and blouses, dresses and hats, coat and dress ensembles with accessories, daytime dresses, and more.

What to look for:

Although she is often dismissed as one of the little hard plastic dolls readily available, you should check your garage sales for Sandra Sue, and her collectible wardrobe. Dolls should be clean, have original clothing, and good facial coloring. Her original box is easily recognizable with a silhouette in an oval and her name marked on top.

8" hard plastic triplet Sandra Sue dolls in box with holder for three dolls, all flat feet, in slip, two blonde, one with reddish wigged, circa 1954, $600.00.
Courtesy Amy Thompson.

Roldan

Roldan characters are similar to Klumpe figures in many respects. They were made in Barcelona, Spain, from the early 1960s until the mid-1970s. They are made of felt over a wire armature, with painted mask faces. Like Klumpe, Roldan figures represent professionals, hobbyists, dancers, historical characters, and contemporary males and females performing a wide variety of tasks. Some, but not all Roldans, were imported by Rosenfeld Imports and Leora Dolores of Hollywood. Figures originally came with two sewn on, identifying cardboard tags. Roldan characters most commonly found are doctors, Spanish dancers, and bull fighters. Roldan characters tend to have somewhat smaller heads, longer necks, and more defined facial features than Klumpe.

What to look for:

Look for bright and clean doll tags; the more accessories, the more collectible these whimsical characters are.

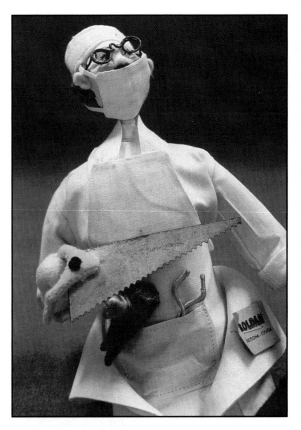

10" felt Sawbones with Roldan paper tag, circa 1960s, $125.00. *Courtesy Sharon Kolibaba.*

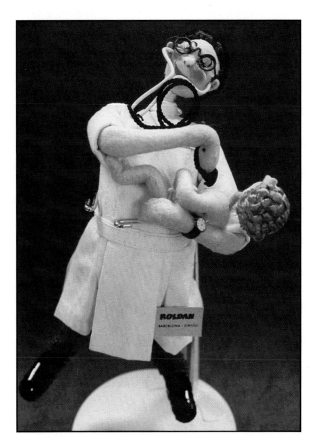

9½" felt cloth doctor character, with Roldan marked paper tag, circa 1960s, $125.00. *Courtesy Sharon Kolibaba.*

Sasha

Sasha dolls were created by Swiss artist, Sasha Morgenthaler, who handcrafted 20" children and 13" babies in Zurich, Switzerland, from the 1940s until her death in 1975. Her handmade studio dolls had cloth or molded bodies, five different head molds, and were hand painted by Sasha Morganthaler. To make her dolls affordable as children's playthings, she licensed Gotz Puppenfabric (1964 – 1970) in Germany and Frido Trendon Ltd. (1965 – 1986) in England to manufacture 16" Sasha dolls in series. The manufactured dolls were made of rigid vinyl with painted features. Gotz Dolls, Inc. was granted a new license in 1994 and is currently producing them in Germany. See Collectors' Network for more information on the Sasha newsletter.

What to look for:

These winsome little children are delightful to add to your collection. Sasha's dolls are found in rigid vinyl in several body shapes. The Trendon Ltd. doll has a jointed socket head, painted features, and some wear. They are unmarked except for a printed round card in a metal ring attached to doll's wrist. They have rooted nylon hair, a closed mouth, and flat feet that enable child doll to stand.

16" vinyl Sari with black hair, played with, hair cut, only 400 made of this model, circa 1986, $95.00. *Courtesy Olivina Mata.*

16" vinyl Gotz Sasha dressed as European Girl Scout, circa 1960s, recent German Sashas in original outfits sold at auction $1,200.00 to $2,200.00. *Courtesy Dorisanne Osborn.*

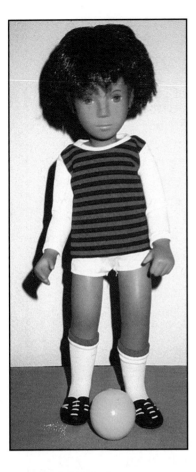

16" vinyl Gregor #303, stripe sport set, all original, MIB, circa 1982, $300.00.
Courtesy Sue Robertson.

16" vinyl Gregor in crayon tube, denims; and 16" vinyl Sasha in pink dress, also in crayon tube, circa 1969 – 1972, $275.00 each.
Courtesy McMasters Doll Auctions.

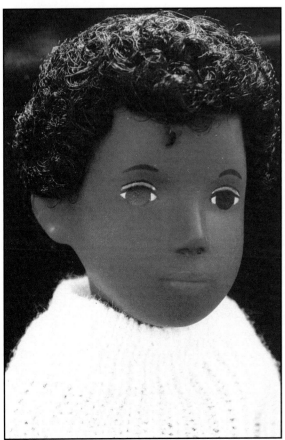

16" vinyl early first Caleb with wrist tag, dark brown features, $175.00.
Courtesy Sally DeSmet.

16" vinyl Sasha, blue checked gingham dress, in tube, brunette, $225.00. *Courtesy Sally DeSmet.*

Shirley Temple

In 1934, after Shirley Temple stole the show with her performance in *Stand Up and Cheer,* Ideal gained the license to produce Shirley Temple dolls, hired Bernard Lipfert to sculpt a prototype, cast her in composition, and soon had Shirley Temple dolls in red and white polka dotted dresses on the market. The costumes were designed by Mollye Goldman from 1934 to 1936, and show the NRA markings on their labels. The costumes were sold separately as well as with the doll. The composition dolls had sleep eyes, with some flirty eyes, open mouth with six upper teeth, multi-stroke eyebrows, a five-piece jointed body, mohair wig, and soon came in a range of sizes from 11" to 27". The first dolls were packaged with a pinback button and signed photograph. Marked on the head and/or torso, was *SHIRLEY TEMPLE//IDEAL NOV. & TOY CO.* with *SHIRLEY TEMPLE* on the body. In late 1935, a Shirley Temple Baby was introduced followed by baby carriages and accessories. The Shirley Temple dolls were popular through the early 1940s, declining when Shirley reached adolescence.

In 1957, Ideal reissued a vinyl 12" Shirley to coincide with the release of her movies to television audiences and as Temple started her own television series. They have plastic script pins and paper hang tags. In the 1960s, 15", 17", and 19" vinyl dolls were issued. In 1972, Montgomery Wards, to celebrate its 100th anniversary, issued a 15" vinyl Shirley Temple. In 1982, Ideal made 8" and 12" Shirley Temple dolls costumed as *Heidi, Stowaway, Stand Up and Cheer, The Little Colonel, Captain January,* and *The Littlest Rebel.* Danbury Mint has made more recent Shirley Temple dolls, including porcelain 20" dolls designed by Elke Hutchens and costumed from movies. See Collectors' Network for information on several Shirley Temple publications and groups.

What to look for:

Composition Shirley Temples are difficult to find in excellent condition because the painted finish crazes, and so those in very good condition have risen drastically in price. Collectors may wish to search for the vinyl and newer dolls as they, too, will eventually become collectible. Check composition dolls for crazing, vinyls should have good color, and clothing should be clean and bright. Shirley collectors like all Shirley Temple related items such as marked products, paper, and advertising.

Composition

Composition Ideal Shirley Temple pair in original boxes, both in coin dot *Stand Up and Cheer* dresses; left: 17", unplayed with condition, pin-back button, in blue, $1,500.00; right: 18½", circa 1934+, $1,500.00. *Courtesy Rachel R. Quigley.*

13" composition Ideal Shirley Temple in tagged plaid *Bright Eyes* dress, clear eyes, slight crazing on composition, circa 1934, $795.00.
Courtesy Leslie Tannenbaum.

18" composition Ideal Shirley Temple original *Bright Eyes* costume, sleep eyes, open mouth, teeth, circa 1934+, $875.00.
Courtesy Iva Mae Jones.

13" composition Ideal Shirley Temple, all original tagged navy sailor suit, pinback button, costume from *Captain January* 1936 movie, circa 1936, plus three more tagged original outfits and Shirley Temple trunk, $1,500.00.
Courtesy Rachel R. Quigley.

13" composition Ideal Shirley Temple, all original in tagged navy sailor suit, original pin-back button, costume from *Captain January* 1936 movie, circa 1936, $1,000.00. *Courtesy Rachel R. Quigley.*

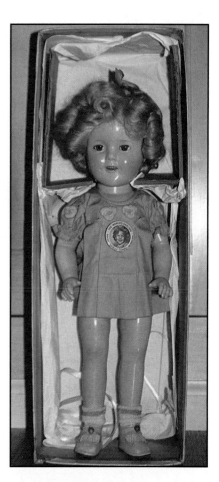

16" composition Ideal Shirley Temple tagged blue *Curly Top* dress, pin, original box, clear eyes, no crazing, circa 1935, $1,250.00. *Courtesy Leslie Tannenbaum.*

18" composition Ideal Shirley Temple, original box (not shown), in tagged original *Curly Top* party dress with pin, eyes and composition only slightly crazed, circa 1935, $1,300.00. *Courtesy Leslie Tannenbaum.*

18" composition Ideal Shirley Temple, original box (not shown), in tagged original *Curly Top* party dress with pin, eyes and composition slightly crazed, circa 1935, $1,500.00. *Courtesy Leslie Tannenbaum.*

13" composition Ideal Shirley Temple with tagged dress, circa 1934+, $700.00.
Courtesy Jane Foster.

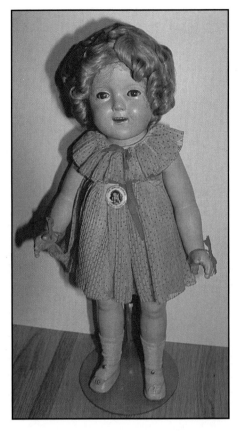

25" composition Ideal Shirley Temple, flirty eyes, original pin, original red and white *Curly Top* party dress, slight crazing to composition and eyes, circa 1935, $1,000.00.
Courtesy Leslie Tannenbaum.

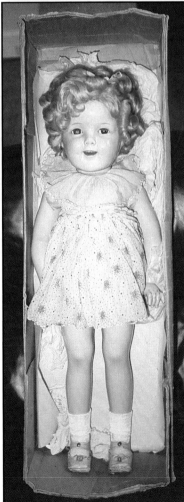

27" composition Ideal Shirley Temple, boxed, tagged knife pleated pink and brown starburst pattern *Curly Top* dress, circa 1934+, $2,000.00.
Courtesy Rachel R. Quigley.

20" composition Ideal Shirley Temple with open mouth, sleep eyes, mohair wig, aqua starburst pattern party dress, circa 1934+, $1,000.00.
Courtesy Iva Mae Jones.

Shirley Temple

Left to right: 25" composition Ideal Shirley Temple, original dress, pinback button, $1,300.00; 13" composition Shirley Temple in tagged *Curly Top* dress, $700.00; and 27" composition Shirley Temple in sunburst print party dress, $1,400.00; circa 1934+. *Courtesy Jane Foster.*

13" composition Ideal Shirley Temple wearing *Curly Top* party dress, extra outfits, trunk, and key, unplayed with condition, circa 1934+, $1,500.00. *Courtesy Rachel R. Quigley.*

18" composition Ideal Shirley Temple, mint-in-box, green sleep eyes, open mouth, teeth, dimples, mohair wig, uncommon red dress, original pin, circa 1934+, $950.00. *Courtesy Iva Mae Jones.*

18" composition Ideal Shirley Temple, eyes and composition slightly crazed, original tagged green party dress, pin, dark blue velvet coat and hat, untagged, possibly original, ST child's handbag, circa 1935+, **$900.00.** *Courtesy Leslie Tannenbaum.*

20" composition Ideal Shirley Temple in pink taffeta *Little Colonel* costume, replaced bows, flowers, circa 1935+, **$1,800.00.**
Courtesy Rachel R. Quigley.

18" composition Ideal Shirley Temple in blue floral print *Littlest Rebel* hard to find costume, with pin, circa 1935, **$1,800.00.**
Courtesy Iva Mae Jones.

18" composition Ideal Shirley Temple, all original tagged yellow print dress, with white organdy pinafore costume from *The Littlest Rebel* movie, circa 1935+, $950.00.
Courtesy Rachel R. Quigley.

13" composition Ideal Shirley Temple in *The Littlest Rebel* costume from 1935 movie, all original, sleep eyes, open mouth, teeth, dimples, mohair wig, original pin, circa 1935, $625.00.
Courtesy Iva Mae Jones.

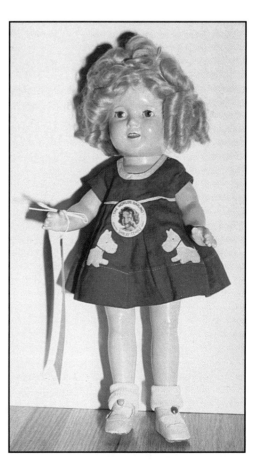

16" composition Ideal Shirley Temple in *The Littlest Rebel* tagged pink print dress with pinafore with pin, eyes crazed, composition perfect, original set mohair wig, circa 1935, $800.00.
Courtesy Leslie Tannenbaum

13" composition Ideal Shirley Temple, clear eyes, very little crazing, tagged Scottie dog dress with pin, circa 1935, $995.00.
Courtesy Leslie Tannenbaum.

16" composition Ideal Shirley Temple in Scottie dog tagged NRA dress, circa 1934 – 1936, $625.00. *Courtesy McMasters Doll Auctions.*

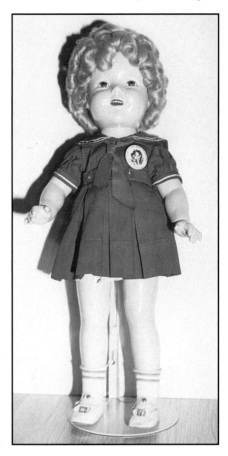

20" composition Ideal Shirley Temple in original tagged sailor dress with pin, eyes clear, slight crazing on composition, circa 1934+, $1,100.00. *Courtesy Leslie Tannenbaum.*

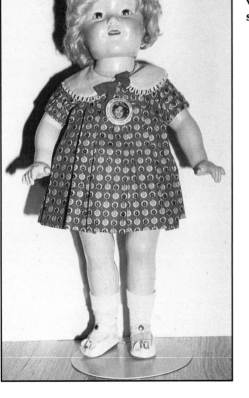

18" composition Ideal Shirley Temple, original red print tagged outfit with pin, eyes and composition slightly crazed, circa 1934+, $1,000.00. *Courtesy Leslie Tannenbaum.*

16" composition Ideal Shirley Temple, clear eyes, yellow tagged dress, slight crazing, circa 1934+, $900.00. *Courtesy Leslie Tannenbaum.*

25" composition Ideal Shirley Temple, all original tagged costume, pin, *Wee Willie Winkie* movie, hard-to-find blue traveling outfit, flirty eyes, circa 1937, $2,000.00. *Courtesy Rachel R. Quigley.*

From left to right: three 18" composition Ideal Shirley Temples: tagged red print 1936 *Poor Little Rich Girl* dress, fur coat, extras/trunk, $1,600.00+; yellow print 1935 *The Littlest Rebel*, $975.00; 1934 *Curly Top*, $750.00. *Courtesy Rachel R. Quigley.*

18" composition Ideal Shirley Temple, all original, sleep eyes, open mouth, teeth, dimples, mohair wig, blue dress with white polka dots, tagged, rayon dress tag, original pin, circa 1934+, $850.00. *Courtesy Iva Mae Jones.*

18" composition Ideal Shirley
Temple, all original, brown sleep
eyes, open mouth, teeth, dimples, mohair wig, dressed in
white fur coat, circa 1934+,
$850.00. *Courtesy Iva Mae Jones.*

27" composition Ideal Shirley Temple in Texas
Ranger/Cowgirl, real leather vest and chaps,
original clothes, replaced felt hat, holster, and
gun, outfit was designed for the 1936 Texas
Centennial celebration, circa 1936, $1,100.00.
Courtesy Iva Mae Jones.

18" composition Shirley Temple dressed
in original peach organdy dress with
white leaf design, original Shirley pinback
button, circa 1939, $1,150.00.
Courtesy McMasters Doll Auctions.

13" composition Ideal Shirley Temple, all original with pin, dress tagged *A Genuine Shirley Temple Doll Dress,* light blue dress, dark blue ribbon around waist with bows on sleeves, shoes, white socks, circa 1935, $350.00. *Courtesy Iva Mae Jones.*

36" tall x 24" wide x 24" deep Shirley Temple pipe organ doll display made by Herbert O. Brown of Fairfield, Maine, circa 1938, with re-dressed Shirley Temple doll, $3,500.00. *Courtesy Iva Mae Jones.*

Ideal used a Shirley Temple dolls for this 16" composition Snow White at pipe organ, original print dress, velvet cape, with original packing box, label, light crazing, circa 1939, $800.00. *Courtesy McMasters Doll Auctions.*

13" composition Ideal Marama, painted eyes to side, open/closed smiling mouth, four painted upper teeth, black yarn hair, hula skirt, circa 1940, $600.00. *Courtesy McMasters Doll Auctions.* A Shirley Temple doll was used by Ideal for the Marama character from the movie *Hurricane* but Shirley Temple did not play the character. Even so, the doll remains a favorite with Shirley collectors.

Left: 20½" composition Ideal Baby Shirley Temple, flirty eye, open mouth, in original dress, circa 1935+, $1,250.00; right: 16" composition Ideal Baby Shirley Temple, flirty eyes, open mouth, original dress, circa 1935+, $1,200.00. *Courtesy Rachel R. Quigley.*

16" composition Ideal Baby Shirley Temple, flirty eyes, tagged original outfit, pin, circa 1935+, $1,200.00; wooden Shirley Temple doll buggy, with marked hubcaps, and photo logo decals, hood torn, circa 1935, $600.00. *Courtesy Leslie Tannenbaum.*

22" composition Reliable Shirley Temple, original *The Littlest Rebel* outfit, sold in Canada, circa 1936+, $500.00. *Courtesy McMasters Doll Auctions.*

Vinyl

12" vinyl Ideal Shirley Temple, all original in pale aqua and white nylon party dress with white lace, original hat and wrist tag, circa 1957, $235.00. *Courtesy Iva Mae Jones.*

12" vinyl Ideal Shirley Temple, all original, lavender dress, tagged Shirley Temple white organdy apron, shoes and socks replaced, circa 1957, $200.00. *Courtesy Iva Mae Jones.*

12" vinyl Shirley Temple, all original with box, script pin, purse, in red and white dress, circa 1957+, $235.00. *Courtesy Rachel R. Quigley.*

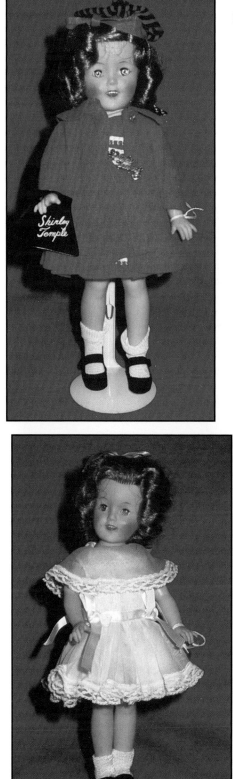

12" vinyl Ideal Shirley Temple, all original, hair in original set, circa 1957, $200.00.
Courtesy Millie Carol.

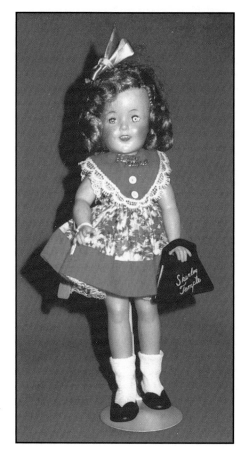

12" vinyl Ideal Shirley Temple, all original, circa 1957, $250.00.
Courtesy Millie Carol.

12" vinyl Ideal Shirley Temple, all original, circa 1957, $250.00.
Courtesy Millie Carol.

12" vinyl Ideal Shirley Temple in original box, with four extra outfits, hang tag, roller skates, circa 1957+, $600.00.
Courtesy Leslie Tannenbaum.

12" Ideal 1957 vinyl Shirley Temple, boxed, in *Wee Willie Winkie* outfit, circa 1957, $600.00. *Courtesy McMasters Doll Auctions.*

12" vinyl Ideal Shirley Temple dressed in original tagged pink taffeta slip and panties, with original box, script Shirley pin, hair in the original set, circa 1957, $400.00. *Courtesy McMasters Doll Auction.*

12" vinyl Ideal Shirley Temple in black top hat, black riding jacket with English flag on left lapel, cream knit jodhpurs, molded black boots, riding crop, circa 1957, $225.00. *Courtesy Iva Mae Jones.* This costume is unknown to Shirley collectors and may have some English connections.

12" vinyl Ideal Shirley Temple,
original velveteen dress, tagged,
replaced shoes and socks, circa
1957, $200.00.
Courtesy Iva Mae Jones.

15" vinyl Shirley Temple dressed as Alice
in Wonderland, all original, sleep eyes,
rare doll, circa 1958 – 1961, $300.00.
Courtesy Iva Mae Jones.

15" vinyl Ideal Shirley Temple dressed
in original blue print dress with lace
and black velvet ribbon trim, hazel
sleep eyes, open mouth with six upper
teeth, circa 1958+, $195.00.
Courtesy McMasters Doll Auctions.

15" vinyl Ideal Shirley Temple in red
and white Cinderella costume with
crown, only available through catalogs, all original, circa 1961, $375.00.
Courtesy Rachel R. Quigley.

15" vinyl Ideal Shirley Temple, boxed, in *Wee Willie Winkie*
movie costume, lovely color, circa 1958, $400.00.
Courtesy Rachel R. Quigley.

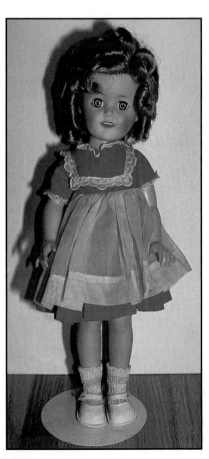

15" vinyl Ideal Shirley Temple, high
cheek color, possible original red
dress with white overskirt, untagged,
circa 1958 – 1961, $150.00.
Courtesy Leslie Tannenbaum.

15" vinyl Ideal Shirley Temple, original
pink shadow design outfit, purse, name
pin, hang tag, high cheek color, hair in
original set, circa 1958 – 1961, $350.00.
Courtesy Leslie Tannenbaum.

16" vinyl Shirley Temple in red dot *Stand Up and
Cheer* outfit, in picture box, circa 1973, $165.00.
Courtesy Iva Mae Jones.

15" vinyl Shirley Temple, all original,
dressed in red print cotton dress with
attached slip and undies to match,
hair net, shoes are marked *Ideal Toy
Corp. 14,* circa 1958 – 1961, $175.00.
Courtesy Iva Mae Jones.

15" vinyl Ideal Shirley Temple,
all original, flirty eyes, hair net,
pale pink dress with light blue
ribbon sash, circa 1960,
$400.00. *Courtesy Iva Mae Jones.*

15" vinyl Ideal Shirley Temple, mint in
box, #1410, dressed as *Captain January,*
sleep eyes, net on hair, script pin, fully
jointed, all original tagged dress and hat,
circa 1958 – 1961, $350.00.
Courtesy Iva Mae Jones.

17" vinyl Ideal Shirley Temple in
unusual original tagged black bodice
and red trim outfit, high cheek
color, circa 1958 – 1961, $400.00.
Courtesy Leslie Tannenbaum.

17" vinyl Ideal Shirley Temple with paper wrist tag in original box with silver script pin, dressed in *Wee Willie Winkie* outfit, circa 1958 – 1961, $575.00. *Courtesy McMasters Doll Auctions.*

17" vinyl Ideal Shirley Temple, original tagged red sailor type outfit with purse, high cheek color, circa 1958 – 1961, $400.00. *Courtesy Leslie Tannenbaum.*

17" vinyl Ideal Shirley Temple in original oufit, with pin, purse, hang tag, circa 1958 – 1961, $550.00. *Courtesy Leslie Tannenbaum.*

Shirley Temple

17" vinyl Ideal Shirley Temple, mint-in-box, tagged fuchsia color original dress with white organdy apron, Shirley Temple pin, pocketbook, socks and shoes, with original owner provenance, circa 1958 – 1961, $695.00. *Courtesy Iva Mae Jones.*

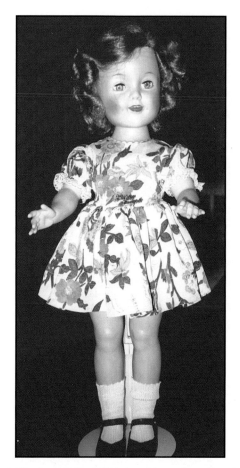

19" vinyl Ideal Shirley Temple, all original, sleep eyes, unusual tagged dress of flowered sharkskin taffeta, circa 1958 – 1961, $400.00.
Courtesy Iva Mae Jones.

19" vinyl Ideal Shirley Temple re-dressed in *Wee Willie Winkie* costume, flirty eyes, circa 1957, $350.00.
Courtesy Millie Carol.

19" vinyl Ideal Shirley Temple,
original tagged white dotted Swiss
outfit, original hair set, high cheek
color, circa 1958 – 1961, $400.00.
Courtesy Leslie Tannenbaum.

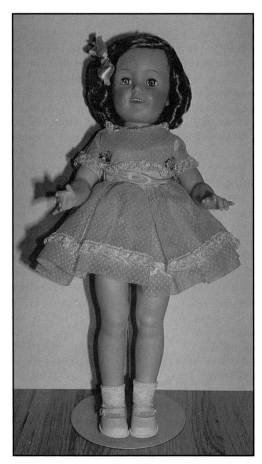

Left: 19" vinyl Shirley Temple, flirty eyes, in
red and black tagged dress, circa 1958 –
1961, $400.00; right: 17" vinyl Ideal Shirley
Temple, flirty eyes, in *Wee Willie Winkie* costume, circa 1958 – 1961, $375.00.
Courtesy Rachel R. Quigley.

19" vinyl Ideal Shirley Temple,
all original in tagged blue dress,
circa 1958 – 1961, $425.00.
Courtesy Iva Mae Jones.

Shirley Temple

19" vinyl Ideal Shirley Temple Walker, all original, brown sleep eyes, pink cotton dress with white pinafore in organdy with three rows of lace, script pin, black purse, circa 1958 – 1961, $485.00. *Courtesy Iva Mae Jones.*

Six 12" vinyl MIB Ideal Shirley Temple dolls, 1982, and six 1983 Ideal Shirley Temple dolls in original boxes, hang tags, $35.00+ each. *Courtesy Leslie Tannenbaum.*

16" vinyl Danbury Mint Shirley Temple with 18 original costumes which sold for $33.00 each, doll and costumes, circa 1990s, $600.00. *Courtesy Millie Carol.*

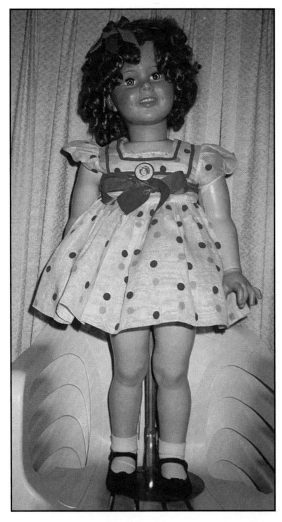

35" vinyl Ideal Shirley Temple, all original, with jointed wrists, uses Playpal body, rosy cheek color, well kept hair, nylon dress with pink floral decoration, circa 1960, $1,500.00. *Courtesy Rachel R. Quigley.*

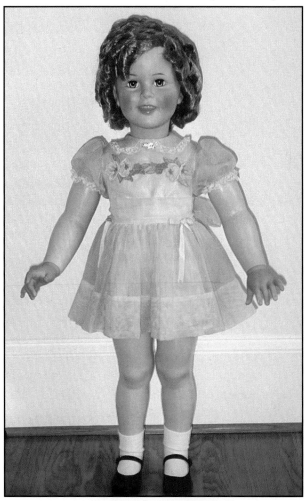

36" vinyl Ideal Shirley Temple, vinyl hands with jointed wrists, rigid vinyl body, rooted saran hair, sleep eyes, open/closed mouth with teeth, dimples, circa 1960, $2,000.00. *Courtesy Millie Busch.*

12" plaster bust of Shirley Temple by F. Coffin, perhaps used as a jewelry display, circa 1930 – 1940s, $1,200.00. *Courtesy Iva Mae Jones.*

Terri Lee

Terri Lee was made from 1946 to 1962, in Lincoln, Nebraska, and Apple Valley, California. Dolls were first made of composition, then hard plastic and vinyl. They had closed pouty mouths, painted eyes, wigs, and jointed bodies. They were marked on torso, *TERRI LEE* and the early dolls were marked *PAT. PENDING.*

Recently the molds were acquired to remake Terri Lee dolls, but the company was barred from doing so by legal action from heirs of the founder. See Collectors' Network for more information on collector groups and the bibliography for additional resource material.

What to look for:

Composition dolls are hard to find in good condition as most have crazing in moderate to severe stages. Hard plastic dolls should be clean with rosy face color and original clothing when possible. Hair can be restyled and clothes made for nude dolls. Again a stable environment and cleanliness is needed to avoid deterioration of the plastic materials.

16" black composition Terri Lee Patty Jo in Calypso tagged outfit, unplayed with condition, circa 1950s, $1,300.00.
Courtesy McMasters Doll Auctions.

16" hard plastic Terri Lee in pink formal, platinum blonde slightly disheveled, painted features, circa 1951 – 1962, $325.00.
Courtesy Darleen Foote.

**16" hard plastic Terri Lee Bride
with original tagged dress, painted
features, brown wig slightly
disheveled, circa 1951 – 1962,
$325.00.** *Courtesy Darleen Foote.*

**Three 16" Terri Lee dolls, left: hard plastic, circa 1951+,
$400.00; center: soft stuffed vinyl-type, circa 1947, $800.00;
and right: in heart fund dress, painted hard plastic, wearing
Heart Fund dress, circa 1947 – 1950, $475.00.**
Courtesy Angie Gonzales.

**16" unmarked soft plastic Terri Lee,
believed to be a prototype as the company tested different materials with
stuffed softer plastic, circa 1947,
$800.00.** *Courtesy Angie Gonzales.*

Terri Lee

16" hard plastic Terri Lee, fully jointed, painted eyes, blonde wig, circa 1952 – 1962, $200.00. *Courtesy Cathie Clark.*

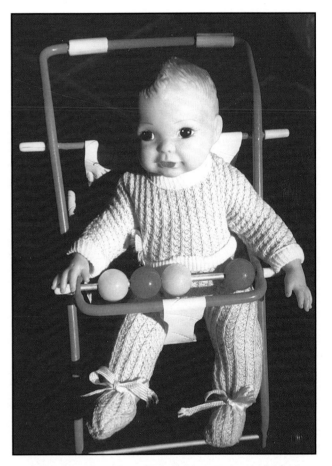

10" vinyl Terri Lee Linda Lee Baby, molded blonde hair, brown painted eyes, original pink crocheted footed nightie trimmed in white, pink metal stroller, circa 1952 – 1958, $185.00. *Courtesy Iva Mae Jones.*

10" vinyl Tiny Terri Lee, painted molded features, long white christening dress, circa 1955 – 1958, $150.00. *Courtesy Catherine Shupe.*

Travel Dolls

A new trend in collectibles has emerged over the past few years with the concept of the travel doll. This is a revival of an earlier concept of pocket dolls, small dolls that could be tucked into a pocket or bag and brought out when the child needed to be amused. Retired librarian, Adele Leurquin, while researching fashion articles in turn-of-the-century fashion magazines, came across an article about travel dolls. The doll was taken only on trips or excursions and put away when returning home. She brought the idea to her club and they all found small dolls and began sewing for them.

There are no hard and fast rules for the dolls, but some guidelines are mentioned. Travel dolls are usually small dolls so they can be easily carried. You may wish to choose a 4½" to 9" tall doll. Your travel doll can be of any material, old or new, bisque, hard plastic, composition, vinyl, wood, or other material. It is nice if your travel doll has jointed legs so that she can sit without a doll stand when you take her to club meetings, luncheons, conventions, or on trips. It is nice to have a container such as a trunk or suitcase to carry your travel doll, her accessories, and wardrobe. Some have been quite creative when choosing trunks; Patches, a travel bear, makes his home in his own wooden "ammo" case.

It is fun to record your travel doll's experiences in a journal so that you can keep track of what is happening to her. This concept is just for fun, a way to be creative and express your own ideas without having to conform to any rules or regulations and is particularly enjoyed by those who like to create wardrobes. Travel dolls can have a new costume for each new trip to reflect where they have traveled. Because the doll is small, it can be taken on extended trips in motor homes, trains, or automobiles. This is a concept — so you can improvise with your own personal choices and it still remains a great idea for amusing a child (or an adult) when traveling.

What to look for:

Here is where you can do your own thing. There are no hard and fast rules. You can choose any type of doll (or bear) and outfit a carrying case for her in any theme you choose.

Dee Cermak chose this 7¾" bisque Armand Marseille circa 1900+ girl, marked only with size number and AM, with composition body. A similar AM might be found nude for $125.00. Wardrobe or accessories increase value to $500.00+.

Vinyl Dolls

By the mid-fifties, vinyl (polyvinylchloride) was being used for dolls. Material that is soft to the touch and processing that allowed hair to be rooted are positive attractions. Vinyl has become a desirable material and the market has been deluged with dolls manufactured from this product. Many dolls of this period are of little known manufacturer, unmarked, or marked only with a number. With little history behind them, these dolls need to be mint in box and totally complete to warrant top prices. An important factor to remember when purchasing vinyl dolls: all aspects of originality, labeled costume, hang tag, and box are more critical when these dolls are entered into competition.

What to look for:

Clean dolls, all original with good color, vinyl that is not sticky. There can be some real bargains in this area for the collector with a limited budget. Often overlooked character and celebrity dolls in vinyl can still be found at garage sales, flea markets, discount outlets, and antique malls.

Baby/Toddler

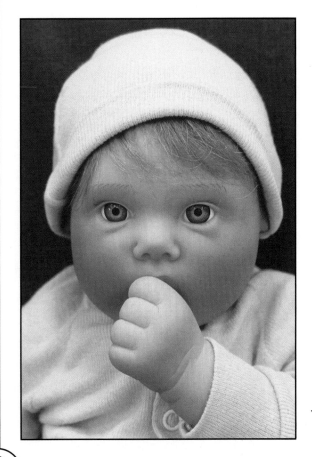

15" vinyl Correlle limited edition signed by Catherine Refabery, made in France, ball and socket vinyl limbs, circa 1990s, $200.00. *Courtesy Connie Lee Martin.*

18½" vinyl Lee Middleton Honey Loves awake girl, with glass eyes, open/closed mouth to accept thumb or pacifier, synthetic wig, cloth weighted body, vinyl feet and hands, blue infant outfit, 1996+, $120.00. *Courtesy Kim Shelton.*

18½" vinyl Lee Middleton Honey Loves awake girl, with glass eyes open/closed mouth to accept thumb or pacifier, synthetic wig, cloth weighted body, vinyl feet and hands, pink infant outfit, 1996+, $120.00. *Courtesy Brenda Shelton.*

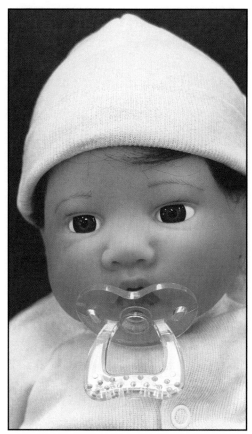

12" all-vinyl Tyco Baby Feels So Real, circa 1991, $20.00. *Courtesy Marie Rodgers.*

16½" vinyl Tyco Twinkling Thumbelina with blonde rooted hair, glass eyes, original tagged outfit, hard to find with rattle that inserts into hand, battery operated, doll moves, rattle lights, circa 1991, $45.00. *Courtesy Marie Rodgers.*

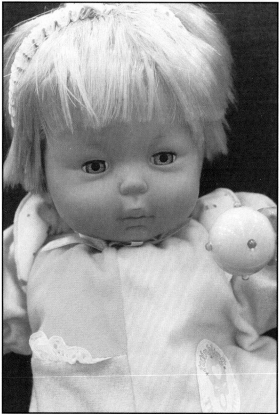

Vinyl Dolls

16" vinyl Uneeda toddler, rigid vinyl body, circa 1981, $25.00. *Courtesy Connie Baca.*

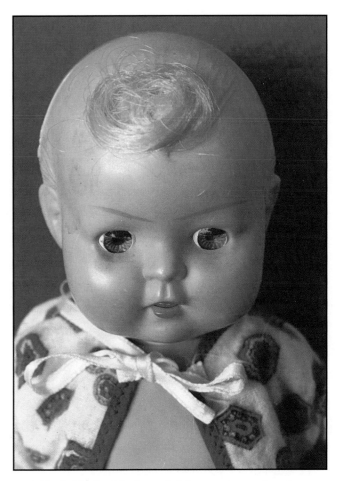

10" rigid vinyl baby with inset eyes, glued on forelock, had world globe mark, circa 1980s, $30.00. *Private collection.*

22" vinyl Italian baby, tagged Zanini & Zambelli, 1984 limited edition, $95.00. *Courtesy Laura Jennine Jacobs.*

Child/Adult

10" vinyl ethnic boy and girl, Goebel Hummel types in ethnic costume, with molded hair, painted eyes, original costume, circa 1952, $25.00 each.
Courtesy Jill McMorran.

6½" vinyl Furga toddler, with original red coat outfit and hang tag, circa 1960s, $45.00.
Courtesy Sharon Kolibaba.

28" rigid vinyl Furga lady doll with fancy long dress of synthetic material, mohair wig, sleep eyes, gaudy trim, circa 1961, $150.00. *Courtesy Mary Jane Franz.*

**8" vinyl Kehagias Alice in Won-
derland, made in Greece, all
original, circa 1980s, $35.00.**
Courtesy Millie Busch.

**18" vinyl Magic Attic Alison designed by
Robert Tonner, circa 1997, $69.00, wears
extra bridesmaid outfit, $24.00.**
Courtesy Millie Carol.

**18" vinyl Magic Attic Rose in
original Magic Attic cos-
tume, circa 1997, $60.00.**
Courtesy Millie Busch.

11" vinyl Paris Doll Corp. Jaci, closed mouth, turquoise plastic sleep eyes, jointed vinyl body, designed by 12-year-old Jaci Barrett, brochure shows *Parents* magazine approval seal, original skating dress and cap, circa 1956, $15.00. *Courtesy Penny Hustler.*

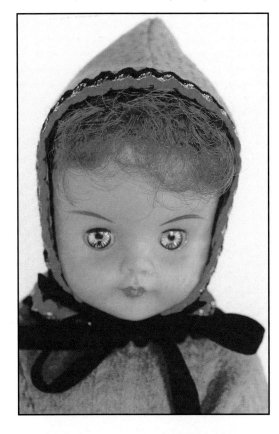

24" vinyl black Play-mates Cricket, all original in box, talk-er with recorder, circa 1985, $125.00. *Courtesy Pauline Lyon.*

18" vinyl Pleasant Company American Girl Josephina, sleep eyes, open/closed mouth with two teeth, black synthetic wig, cloth body, vinyl limbs, Christmas dress with her doll and chicken and chilies, circa 1997, basic doll with book, $82.00. *Private collection.*

11" vinyl Sayco Miss America Pageant with rigid vinyl body, all original, with two mint-in-box outfits, circa 1950 – 1960s, $175.00. *Courtesy Pam Martinec.*

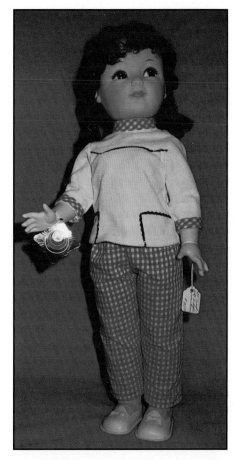

19" vinyl child with hang tag reading *Shanghai Toys Factory #7//Made in China,* circa 1991, $50.00. *Courtesy Millie Carol.*

18" rigid vinyl Tomy Kimberly, original cheerleader outfit, with skates, circa 1980s, $40.00. *Courtesy Marie Rodgers.*

11" vinyl Uneeda Dollikin, jointed
arms, legs, feet, and waist, marked
*Uneeda Doll Co.
Inc.//MCMLX//Made in Hong Kong,*
circa 1960, $55.00.
Courtesy Carol Bennett.

18" vinyl Valentine, high-heel girl with
sleep eyes, rooted synthetic wig, rigid vinyl
body, original strapless net formal with
marked Valentine box, circa 1950s, $95.00.
Courtesy Penny Pittsley.

15" vinyl Uneeda Granny and
Me, painted on glasses, circa
1990s, $35.00. *Courtesy Lori Rose.*

**17" vinyl girl marked *Wernike KZP 83,*
brown sleep eyes, human hair wig,
jointed elbows, wrists, and knees,
made in West Germany, circa 1990,
$350.00.**
Courtesy Millie Carol.

**18" vinyl World of Wonder Pamela,
cloth body holds cassette player, came
with cassette and book, extra outfits,
circa 1986, $175.00.**
Courtesy Angie Gonzales.

Virga

Virga made hard plastic dolls usually jointed only at the arms and often 7" dolls with inexpensive costumes sold as tourist dolls. In the 1950s, French designer Schiaparelli designed costumes for 12" Virga dolls with vinyl head and hard plastic body. These dolls were marked *Virga* on the head and had a *Schiaparelli* tag in the skirt. Virga also made an 8" Go-Go with vinyl head and hard plastic walker body with Schiaparelli costumes packed in shocking pink box.

8½" hard plastic Lucy Walker in box with shoes, socks, and purse, circa 1950s, $95.00. *Courtesy Sondra Krueger.*

15" vinyl girl, all original, circa 1960s – 1970s, $50.00. *Courtesy Vivian Boucher.*

Vogue

In 1922, Jennie Graves started her Vogue Doll Shop business in Somerville, Massachusetts, by dressing German dolls for department stores. She used cottage industry home sewers as her business expanded. Just before the war, she established a storefront, but depended on home sewers again during the war years, as all able-bodied workers were needed in the defense plants. In 1945, she incorporated Vogue Dolls, Inc., and opened a factory in Medford, Massachusetts. By 1949, she contracted to have an 8" hard plastic doll made with Commonwealth Plastics Company. At no time did she manufacture dolls, but she did open a 15,000 square foot factory where the dolls were dressed and readied for shipment.

Graves designed the costumes for over 20 years. She dressed German Armand Marseille bisque Just Me dolls in early years, and these are highly prized for the costumes today. She also used imported German Kammer & Reinhardt (K*R) dolls to costume and sell as well as composition dolls made by Arranbee and Ideal. In 1937, Graves had doll designer Bernard Lipfert design an 8" composition doll Toddles which she produced until 1948 when she had the doll made in hard plastic named Ginny. In the 1950s, Graves promoted a doll with wardrobe to increase year round sales. Vogue advertising promoted Ginny as a leader in the doll fashion society and noted she had 50 outfits available. This brought such a growth spurt, Graves had to borrow to open another factory in 1953. Her success gave rise to competition such as Ginger by the Cosmopolitan Doll Company. In 1957, Vogue became the largest doll manufacturer in the U.S. In 1958, Vogue purchased Arranbee Doll Company and reported gross sales of over $6 million. Graves retired in 1960 and turned the control of the company over to her daughter Virginia Graves Carlson and son-in-law, Ted Carlson, until 1966 when Virginia retired. In 1972, Vogue was sold to Tonka Corp., who began manufacturing the dolls in Asia. In 1977, the company was purchased by Lesney Products. During the Lesney era the doll was redesigned with a much slimmer body. After several changes of ownership, Meritus (1984) and then R. Dakin in 1986, the rights to Vogue dolls and molds, including Ginny were purchased by Vogue Doll Company, Inc., founded in 1995, by Linda and Jim Smith and Wendy and Keith Lawton (of the Lawton Company) and others. Today President Linda Smith handles marketing while Wendy Lawton oversees designs, making Ginny again a great collectible doll.

What to look for:

Early composition dolls should have minimal crazing and good color. Hard plastic dolls should have good color and original clothing. Hair can be restyled with patience, but clean dolls that have no mold or odor are important considerations. Vogue's Ginny dolls were a big favorite of the baby boomers during the 1950s and remain an appealing collectible with new dolls attracting new as well as older collectors.

Composition

7½" composition Toddles, painted eyes, mohair wig, tagged outfit, circa 1937 – 1948, $200.00.
Courtesy McMasters Doll Auctions.

7½" composition Toddles Dutch pair, all original with silver labels, boxes, circa 1937 – 1948,
$375.00. *Courtesy McMasters Doll Auctions.*

Left: 7½" composition Toddles Uncle Sam, painted eyes to side, closed mouth, original mohair
wig, five-piece composition toddler body, all original, circa 1943 – 1944, $450.00; right: 7½" com-
position Red Riding Hood, painted eyes to side,
closed mouth, original mohair wig, five-piece
composition toddler body, all original, circa 1947,
$275.00. *Courtesy McMasters Doll Auctions.*

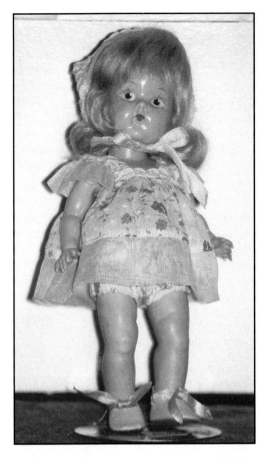

8" composition Toddles, painted features, all original, circa 1937 – 1948, $350.00.
Courtesy Lilian Booth.

Hard Plastic

8" hard plastic Ginny, painted eyes, transitional doll, pink taffeta dress, ink spot tag, circa 1948 – 1950, $300.00. *Courtesy Gay Smedes.*

8" strung hard plastic Ginny Bride, ink spot tag on dress, brown mohair wig, original Bride costume, circa 1948 – 1950, $350.00.
Courtesy Gay Smedes.

8" hard plastic Ginny, painted
eyes, wearing an unidentified
dress, circa 1948 – 1950, $300.00.
Courtesy Cathie Clark.

8" painted hard plastic Ginny dolls, left: in cowgirl
outfit; center: pink outfit; right: Red Riding Hood,
all with painted eyes, circa 1948 – 1950,
$275.00 each. *Courtesy Gay Smedes.*

8" hard plastic Ginny, strung, in
original pink dress with trunk, circa
1951, $500.00.
Courtesy Peggy Millhouse.

8" hard plastic Brother and Sister Ginny dolls, painted lash Steve and Eve, circa 1951, $800.00 for pair.
Courtesy Cathie Clark.

8" hard plastic Ginny, strung, painted lash, wearing the bathing suit to Sport Series, circa 1951, $300.00.
Courtesy Cathie Clark.

8" hard plastic from the Brother and Sister Series, painted lash strung girl named Stina, her brother's name is Sten, circa 1952, $400.00. *Courtesy Cathie Clark.*

8" hard plastic Ginny, strung, painted lash, shown with her original box, circa 1951, $400.00. *Courtesy Cathie Clark.*

7½" hard plastic painted lash Ginny walker, circa 1951 – 1953, two outfits, boxed, $350.00. *Courtesy McMasters Doll Auctions.*

8" hard plastic Kindergarten Series called Kay, strung, painted lash, poodle cut wig in a blue organdy dress with medallion trim, circa 1952, $450.00. *Courtesy Cathie Clark.*

8" hard plastic Ginny, strung, painted lash, dressed as Kay, Kindergarten Series, in a red organdy dress with white medallion shoulder trim, circa 1952, $400.00.
Courtesy Cathie Clark.

8" hard plastic Ginny, strung, painted lash, wearing her pink poodle cloth coat, circa 1952, $400.00.
Courtesy Cathie Clark.

8" hard plastic Ginny, strung, painted lash Square Dance Series in her cotton print with pink trim, circa 1952, $300.00.
Courtesy Cathie Clark.

8" hard plastic Tiny Miss called Cheryl, strung, painted lash, satin dress, gathered lace trim and a pink ribbon sash, shoes are replaced, circa 1952, $400.00.
Courtesy Cathie Clark.

8" hard plastic Ginny, painted lash, poodle
cut wig, in a pink poodle cloth coat and
hat, circa 1952, $400.00.
Courtesy Cathie Clark.

8" hard plastic Ginny roller skater from the
Gad About Series, painted lash, circa 1953,
$400.00. *Courtesy Cathie Clark.*

Three 8" hard plastic Ginny
dolls, painted lash, wearing
Kindergarten Series and Tiny
Miss Series dresses, circa 1952
– 1953, $300.00 each.
Courtesy Cathie Clark.

8" hard plastic Dutch Boy and Girl from the Twin Series, painted lash, both wear wooden shoes and her hat matches her apron, circa 1953, $800.00 pair. *Courtesy Cathie Clark.*

8" hard plastic Ginny as Wanda in her Tiny Miss Series dress, painted lash, missing her blue straw hat, trimmed with cherries, red center snap shoes, circa 1953, $200.00. *Courtesy Cathie Clark.*

8" hard plastic Ginny, painted lash, strung, wearing #29 Tina from the Kindergarten School series, circa 1953, $350.00. *Courtesy Cathie Clark.*

8" hard plastic Ginny, painted lash, in a variation of her beach atttire, circa 1953, $300.00.
Courtesy Cathie Clark.

8" hard plastic Ginny as Angela from the Debutante Series, painted lash, circa 1953, $325.00.
Courtesy Cathie Clark.

8" hard plastic Ginny dolls; #1 skier wearing Funtime Series, painted lash, circa 1954, $400.00; #2 cowgirl Playtime Series, circa 1956, $200.00; #3 skater, Funtime Series, circa 1956, $200.00.
Courtesy Cathie Clark.

Two 8" hard plastic Ginny dolls with painted lashes, strung, in their Sunday best, circa 1954, $250.00 each. *Courtesy Cathie Clark.*

8" hard plastic Ginny Nurse straight-leg walker, circa 1956, $325.00; middle doll is a Merry Moppet School girl, circa 1955, $300.00; and the last one is a Tiny Miss, circa 1954, $275.00. *Courtesy Cathie Clark.*

8" hard plastic Carol, strung, painted lash, in dotted organdy dress from Kindergarten Afternoon Series, circa 1953, $400.00; E-Z DoWardrobe is wooden with cardboard interior, circa 1953 – 1954, $75.00. *Courtesy Cathie Clark.*

8" hard plastic Ginny, sleep eyes, painted lashes, mohair wig, rosy color, straight-leg walker, circa 1954, $275.00. *Courtesy Gay Smedes.*

8" hard plastic Ginny, molded lashes, walker, sleep eyes, aqua Bon Bon #80 dress, circa 1955, $225.00. *Courtesy Peggy Millhouse.*

8" hard plastic Ginny molded lashes, straight-leg walker, wearing Fun Time skating outfit, her skates originally were roller skates, circa 1955, $300.00. *Courtesy Cathie Clark.*

8" hard plastic Ginny molded lashes, straight-leg walker, in an unidentified yellow dress, circa 1955, $100.00.
Courtesy Cathie Clark.

8" hard plastic Ginny, molded lashes, straight-leg walker, wearing a rabbit fur coat, hat, and muff, available in pink, blue, and white, circa 1955, $200.00. *Courtesy Cathie Clark.*

Two 8" hard plastic Ginny dolls molded lashes, straight-leg walkers, red is Kinder Crowd series and green is a Merry Moppit, circa 1956, $200.00 each. *Courtesy Cathie Clark.*

Two 8" hard plastic Ginny dolls in coat, hat, and muff is a molded lashes, straight-leg walker, circa 1955, $200.00; and in her dress, missing apron and clothespins is a bend knee, molded lashes, walker, circa 1957, $150.00. *Courtesy Cathie Clark.*

Three 8" hard plastic Ginny dolls, molded lashes, straight-leg walkers in their original boxes; the skier is from Funtime series; center is a Playtime series doll; and in red is a Deb; circa 1956, $200.00 each.
Courtesy Cathie Clark.

8" hard plastic Ginny sitting on her Dream Cozy bed, circa 1957, bed $30.00, doll $125.00.
Courtesy Cathie Clark.

8" hard plastic Ginny walker
from the Gym Kids Series, bent
knee, molded lashes, circa 1956
and 1957, $150.00.
Courtesy Cathie Clark.

8" hard plastic Ginny, molded lashes, straight-leg walker, wearing her
Hi-Fi fashion gown, circa 1956,
$150.00. *Courtesy Cathie Clark.*

8" hard plastic Ginny molded lashes,
walker, sleep eyes, trunk, hang tag,
five extra outfits plus accessories,
circa 1955 – 1956, $1,100.00+.
Courtesy Rae Klenke.

8" hard plastic Ginny bent-knee walker, molded lashes, blue gown topped with embroidered nylon skirt and lacy straw hat, circa 1957, $150.00. *Courtesy Cathie Clark.*

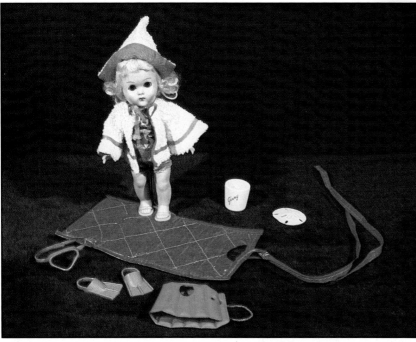

8" hard plastic Ginny, painted lashes, wearing her Funtime Series beach outfit, circa 1954; and playing with her beach accessories, circa 1957 – 1960; doll $300.00.
Courtesy Cathie Clark.

8" vinyl Ginny bent-knee walker, hard plastic body, head does not turn, circa 1963, $40.00; 10½" all hard plastic Jill, wearing a nylon tulle ballerina dress, circa 1957, $200.00. *Courtesy Cathie Clark.*

Vogue

8" hard plastic Ginny straight-leg walker, painted lashes, in blue coat and hat, circa 1954, $400.00; 10½" hard plastic Jill in blue leather coat and hat, circa 1957; Jill in beige Dynel coat/hat, circa 1958; $200.00 each.
Courtesy Cathie Clark.

8" all-vinyl Ginnette sitting on top of her original box, jointed, open mouth, circa 1964, $200.00.
Courtesy Cathie Clark.

8" all-vinyl Ginnette jointed with an open mouth, mint in her original box, circa 1956, $200.00.
Courtesy Cathie Clark.

10½" hard plastic Jill wears Fireside Fashion pants and strapless black velvet top, rabbit shrug, necklace and earrings, circa 1959, $175.00. *Courtesy Cathie Clark.*

10½" hard plastic Jill bent-knee walker, sleep eyes, saran wig, in her Record Hop skirt, circa 1958, $175.00; desk and chair, circa 1958 – 1959, $50.00. *Courtesy Cathie Clark.*

10½" hard plastic Jill, sleep eyes, earrings, wearing Record Hop yellow felt skirt with black jersey top, circa 1958, $175.00. *Courtesy Cathie Clark.*

10½" hard plastic Jill standing in front of her marked Jill-Jan wardrobe, wearing a beige felt sheath skirt and cotton blouse, circa 1958, $175.00.
Courtesy Cathie Clark.

10½" hard plastic Jill bent-knee walker, all jointed, wearing beige twill jodhpurs with a print blouse and brown boots, circa 1958, $175.00.
Courtesy Cathie Clark.

10½" hard plastic Jill, jointed, bent-knee walker, wearing a black felt Record Hop skirt and a red jersey shirt, circa 1957, $175.00.
Courtesy Cathie Clark.

10½" hard plastic Jill, all jointed, bent-knee walker, wearing a beige felt coat with matching hat, circa 1958, $175.00. *Courtesy Cathie Clark.*

Jill and Jan and their bed marked with their names, circa 1959, bed $50.00; Jill and Jan, $125.00 – 175.00 each
Courtesy Cathie Clark.

Two 10½" hard plastic Jill bent-knee walkers, #1 wearing black toreador pants with a white ruffled blouse, red sash, #2 is wearing pink toreador pants and pink blouse with black sash, circa 1957, $175.00 each.
Courtesy Cathie Clark.

10½" hard plastic Jill bent-knee walker, wearing a white lace over toast taffeta sleeveless party dress, circa 1958, $175.00. *Courtesy Cathie Clark.*

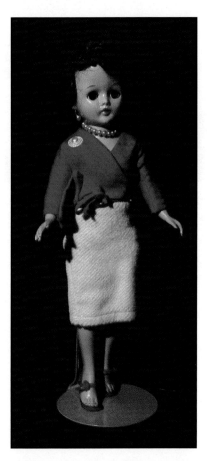

10½" hard plastic Jill wearing a white fleece skirt and a red wrap around blouse, bent-knee walker, sleep eyes, saran wig, circa 1958, $175.00. *Courtesy Cathie Clark.*

Four 10½" hard plastic Jill dolls
at a fashion show, bent-knee
walkers, sleep eyes, saran wig in
either angel cut or pony tail,
circa 1957 – 1960, $175.00 each.
Courtesy Cathie Clark.

11" vinyl Jeff and 10½" hard plastic
Jill and Jan, $125.00 – $150.00 each,
with their bedroom furniture.
Courtesy Cathie Clark.

Two 10½" hard plastic Jill bent-knee
walkers, #1 in a hooded evening
coat with a fur hat and the other in a
black velveteen skirt, circa 1957,
$175.00 each.
Courtesy Cathie Clark.

Vogue

11" all-vinyl Jeff, blue sleep eyes, molded lashes, black painted hair, dances with 10½" hard plastic Jill bent-knee walker, sleep eyes, saran wig, both circa 1958, Jeff, $75.00, Jill, $150.00.
Courtesy Cathie Clark.

11" all-vinyl Jeff, blue sleep eyes, molded lashes, black painted hair, marries 10½" hard plastic Jill bent-knee walker, sleep eyes, saran wig, both circa 1957 – 1959, Jeff, $75.00, Jill, $150.00.
Courtesy Cathie Clark.

10½" hard plastic Jill bent-knee walker, sleep eyes, saran wig, wears a black formal with pink sash, circa 1957, $175.00.
Courtesy Cathie Clark.

10½" hard plastic Jill bent-knee walker with sleep eyes and saran wig, circa 1957, $175.00; and 11" vinyl Jeff, blue sleep eyes, painted hair, circa 1959, $75.00. *Courtesy Cathie Clark.*

10½" all hard plastic Jill bent-knee walker, sleep eyes, saran wig, wearing a pink tulle nylon gown, circa 1959, $200.00. *Courtesy Cathie Clark.*

10½" hard plastic Jill, sleep eyes, bent-knee walker, saran wig, wears black sparkly tutu with pink tulle skirt, circa 1959, $175.00.
Courtesy Cathie Clark.

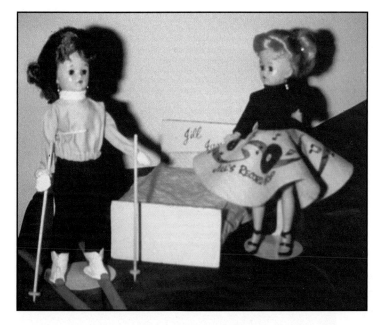

10½" hard plastic Jill, a high-heel doll with adult figure, circa 1957+, $125.00 each in original clothes, bed, $25.00. *Courtesy Mary Fudge.*

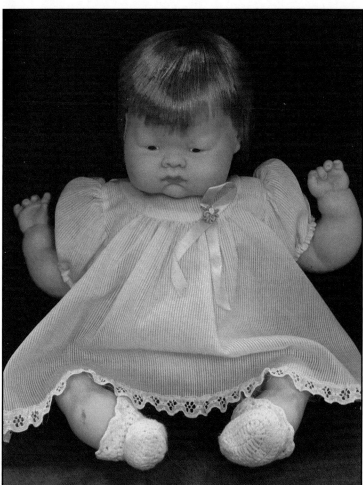

16" vinyl Baby Dear with cloth body, original, circa 1961+, $165.00. *Courtesy Debbie Crume.*

16" vinyl Brikette platinum, rigid vinyl body and legs, ball-jointed twist and turn body, freckles, green sleep eyes, played with, circa 1960, $15.00.
Courtesy Jane Horst.

22" vinyl Brikette with orange hair, freckles, green flirty sleep eyes, an impish character with rigid vinyl body and legs, ball-jointed swivel waist, played with, re-dressed, circa 1959 – 1961, $65.00.
Courtesy Kathy & Roy Smith.

References

No one person can know it all. It is necessary to input data from many sources to bring you this book because of the tremendous scope of this collecting field. With an amazing number of new dolls coming on the market each year and the entire mass of dolls that already exists, more and more collectors are grouping together to share their knowledge and interests. There are clubs, organizations, collectors, Internet chat groups, and others who specializes in one category or type of doll who are willing to talk with others. If you specialize in one of the categories listed in this book and want to share your knowledge with other collectors, please send us your specialty and references or let us know the dolls you would like to see featured.

Collectors' Network

It is strongly recommended when contacting the references below and requesting information that you enclose a SASE (self-addressed stamped envelope) if you wish to receive a reply. Do not ask those who have volunteered to spend money on postage. These collectors may already have many obligations on their time, work schedules, and finances that do not allow them to spend their time and effort to do your research. They might answer if they had an envelope already stamped and addressed.

ALEXANDER DOLL COMPANY
The Review
Official publication of the Madame Alexander
Doll Club
Quarterly, plus two Shoppers
$20.00 per year.
PO Box 330
Mundelein, IL 60060-0330
847-949-9200
Fax: 847-949-9201
Web page: http://www.madc.org

AMERICAN CHARACTER – TRESSY
Debby Davis, Collector/Dealer
3905 N. 15th St.
Milwaukee, WI 53206

ANTIQUE DOLLS
Matrix
PO Box 1410
New York, NY 1002
Can research your wants

ANTIQUE AND MODERN DOLLS
Rosalie Whyel Museum of Doll Art
1116 108th Avenue N.E.
Bellevue, WA 98004
206-455-1116
Fax: 206-455-4793

AUCTION HOUSES:
Call or write for a list of upcoming auctions or if you need information about selling a collection.

McMasters Doll Auctions
James and Shari McMasters
PO Box 1755
Cambridge, OH 43725
800-842-35226
614-432-4419
Fax: 614-432-3191

BARBIE
Miller's Fashion Doll
PO Box 8488
Spokane, WA 99203-0488
509-747-0139
Fax: 509 455-6115
Credit Card Subscription
800-874-5201
Six issues $29.95

Dream Dolls Gallery & More
5700 Okeechobee Blvd. #20
West Palm Beach, FL 33417
888-839-3655
E-mail: dollnmore@aol.com

Jaci Jueden, Collector/Dealer
575 Galice Rd.
Merlin, OR, 97532
E-mail: fudd@cdsnet.net

Steven Pim, Collector/Dealer
3535 17th St.
San Francisco, CA 94110

BETSY MCCALL
Betsy's Fan Club
Marci Van Ausdall, Editor
PO Box 946
Quincy, CA 95971
Quarterly $15.50 per year

CELEBRITY DOLLS
Celebrity Doll Journal
Loraine Burdick, Editor
413 10th Ave. Ct. NE
Puyallup, WA 98372
Quarterly, $10.00 per year

CHATTY CATHY, MATTEL
Chatty Cathy Collector's Club
Lisa Eisenstein, Editor
PO Box 140
Readington, NJ 08870-0140
E-mail: Chatty@eclipse.net
Quarterly Newsletter, $28.00

COMPOSITION AND TRAVEL DOLLS
Effanbee's Patsy Family
Patsy & Friends Newsletter
PO Box 311
Deming, NM 88031
E-mail: patsyandfriends@zianet.com
Bi-monthly, $20.00 per year

COSTUMING
Doll Costumer's Guild
Helen Boothe, Editor
7112 W. Grovers Ave
Glendale, AZ 85308
$16.00 per year, bimonthly

French Fashion Gazette
Adele Leurquin, Editor
1862 Sequoia SE
Port Orchard, WA 98366

DIONNE QUINTUPLETS
Quint News
Jimmy and Fay Rodolfos, Editors
PO Box 2527
Woburn, MA 01888

Connie Lee Martin, Collector/Dealer
4018 East 17th St.
Tucson, AZ, 85711

DOLL REPAIRS
Fresno Doll Hospital
1512 N. College
Fresno, CA 93728
209-266-1108

Kandyland Dolls
PO Box 146
Grande Ronde, OR 97347
503-879-5153

Life's Little Treasures
PO Box 585
Winston, OR 97496
541-679-3472

Oleta's Doll Hospital
1413 Seville Way
Modesto, CA, 95355
209-523-6669

GENE — ASHTON DRAKE GALLERIES
888-For Gene
9200 N. Maryland Ave.
Niles, Il 60714-9853

GIRL SCOUTS
Girl Scout Doll Collectors Patch
Pidd Miller
PO Box 631092
Houston, TX, 77263

Diane Miller, Collector
13151 Roberta Place
Garden Grove, CA 92643

Ann Sutton, Collector/Dealer
2555 Prine Rd.
Lakeland, FL 33810-5703
E-mail: Sydneys@aol.com

HITTY
Friends of Hitty Newsletter
Virginia Ann Heyerdahl, Editor
2704 Bellview Ave
Cheverly, MD 20785
Quarterly, $12.00 per year

Internet, Ebay Auction site
http://cayman.ebay

References

INTERNET LISTS & CHAT ROOMS
AG Collector List
For American Girl, Heidi Ott, and other 18" play dolls,
E-mail: ag_collector_request@lists.best.com

Barbie chat
E-mail: Fashion-l@ga.unc.edu

Doll Chat List
Friendly collectors talk dolls, no flaming permitted,
e-mail is forwarded to your address, no fees.
To subscribe, e-mail: DollChat-Request@nbi.com, type
subscribe in body of message.

Sasha
E-mail: sasha-1-subscribe@makelist.com

Shirley Temple
E-mail: shirleycollect-subscribe@makelist.com

HASBRO - JEM DOLLS
Linda E. Holton, Collector/Dealer
P.O. Box 6753
San Rafael, CA 94903

IDEAL
Ideal Collectors' Newsletter
Judith Izen, Editor
PO Box 623
Lexington, MA 02173
E-mail: Jizen@aol.com
Quarterly, $20.00 per year

KLUMPE DOLLS
Sondra Gast, Collector/Dealer
PO Box 252
Spring Valley, CA 91976
Fax: 619-444-4215

LAWTON, WENDY
Lawton Collectors Guild
PO Box 969
Turlock, CA 95381

Toni Winder, Collector/Dealer
1484 N. Vagedes
Fresno CA 93728
E-mail: TTUK77B@prodigy.com

LIDDLE KIDDLES
For a signed copy of her book, *Liddle Kiddles*
$22.95 post pd., write:
Paris Langford
415 Dodge Ave
Jefferson, LA 70127
504-733-0676

Modern Doll Convention
Cathie Clark, Chairman
2018 Kenton St.
Springfield, OH 45505
513-322-3780

MUSEUMS
Arizona Doll & Toy Museum
602 E. Adams St.
Phoenix, AZ 85004
(Stevens House in Heritage Square)
602-253-9337
Tues – Sun, adm. $2.50, closed Aug.

Enchanted World Doll Museum
"The castle across from the Corn Palace"
615 North Main
Mitchell, SD, 57301
605-996-9896
Fax: 605-996-0210

Land of Enchantment Doll Museum
5201 Constitution Ave.
Albuquerque, NM 87110-5813
505-821-8558
Fax: 505-255-1259

Margaret Woodbury Strong Museum
1 Manhattan Square
Rochester, NY 14607
716-263-2700

Rosalie Whyel Museum of Doll Art
1116 108th Avenue N.E.
Bellevue, WA 98004
206-455-1116
Fax: 206-455-4793
www.dollart.com

NANCY ANN STORYBOOK
Elaine Pardee, Collector/Dealer
PO Box 6108
Santa Rosa, CA 95406
707-585-3655

ORIENTAL DOLLS
Ninsyo Journal - JADE
Japanese American Dolls Enthusiasts
406 Koser Ave
Iowa City, Iowa 52246
E-mail: vickyd@jadejapandolls.com

RAGGEDY ANN
Rags newsletter
Barbara Barth, Editor
PO Box 823
Atlanta, GA 30301
Quarterly $16.00

ROBERT TONNER DOLL COMPANY
Robert Tonner Doll Club
PO Box 1187
Kingston, NY 12402
Credit Card: 914 339-9537
Fax: 914-339-1259
Dues: $19.95

ROLDAN DOLLS
Sondra Gast, Collector/Dealer
PO Box 252
Spring Valley, CA 91976
Fax: 619-444-4215

SANDRA SUE DOLLS, RICHWOOD TOYS INC.
Peggy Millhouse, Collector/Dealer
510 Green Hill Road
Conestoga, PA 17516
E-mail: peggyin717@aol.com

SASHA DOLLS
Friends of Sasha
Quarterly Newsletter
Dorisanne Osborn, Editor
Box 187
Keuka Park, NY 14478

SHIRLEY TEMPLE
Shirley Temple Collectors News
Rita Dubas, Editor
881 Colonial Rd
Brooklyn NY 11209
Quarterly, $20.00 year

Lollipop News
Shirley Temple Collectors By the Sea
PO Box 6203
Oxnard, CA 93031
Membership dues: $14.00 year

TERRI LEE
Daisy Chain Newsletter
Terry Bukowski, Editor
3010 Sundland Dr
Alamogordo, NM 88310
E-mail: bukowski@wazoo.com
$20.00 per year

Ann Sutton, Collector/Dealer
2555 Prine Rd.
Lakeland, FL 33810-5703
E-mail: Sydneys@aol.com

Betty J. Woten, Collector/Dealer
12 Big Bend Cut Off
Cloudcroft, NM 88317-9411

VOGUE
Ginny Doll Club
PO Box 338
Oakdale, CA 95361-0338
800-554-1447

United Federation of Doll Clubs
10920 N. Ambassador Dr., Suite 130
Kansas City, MO, 64153
816-891-7040
Fax: 816-891-8360
http://www.ufdc.org/

WOODS, ROBIN
Toni Winder, Collector/Dealer
1484 N. Vagedes
Fresno, CA 93728

Bibliography

Anderson, Johana Gast. *Twentieth Century Dolls.* Wallace Homestead, 1971.
———. *More Twentieth Century Dolls.* Wallace Homestead, 1974.
———. *Cloth Dolls.* Wallace Homestead, 1984.
Axe, John. *Effanbee, A Collector's Encyclopedia 1949 through 1983.* Hobby House Press, 1983.
———. *The Encyclopedia of Celebrity Dolls.* Hobby House Press, 1983.
———. *Tammy and Her Family of Dolls.* Hobby House Press, 1995.
Blitman, Joe. *Francie & her Mod, Mod, Mod, Mod World of Fashion.* Hobby House Press, 1996.
Casper, Peggy Wiedman. *Fashionable Terri Lee Dolls.* Hobby House Press, 1988.
Crowsey, Linda. *Madame Alexander Collector's Dolls Price Guide #23.* Collector Books, 1998.
Clark, Debra. *Troll Identification & Price Guide.* Collector Books, 1993.
Coleman, Dorthy S., Elizabeth Ann and Evelyn Jane. *The Collector's Book of Dolls Clothes.* Crown Publishers, 1975.
———. *The Collector's Encyclopedia of Dolls, Vol. I & II.* Crown Publishers, 1968, 1986.
DeWein, Sibyl and Ashabraner, Joan. *The Collector's Encyclopedia of Barbie Dolls and Collectibles.* Collector Books, 1977.
Garrison, Susan Ann. *The Raggedy Ann & Andy Family Album.* Schiffer Publishing, 1989.
Hedrick, Susan & Matchette, Vilma. *World Colors, Dolls & Dress.* Hobby House Press, 1997.
Hoyer, Mary. *Mary Hoyer and Her Dolls.* Hobby House Press, 1982.
Izen, Judith. *A Collector's Guide to Ideal Dolls.* Collector Books, 1994.
Izen, Judith and Stover, Carol. *Collector's Encyclopedia of Vogue Dolls.* Collector Books, 1998.
Judd, Polly and Pam. *African and Asian Costumed Dolls.* Hobby House Press, 1995.
———. *Cloth Dolls.* Hobby House Press, 1990.
———. *Composition Dolls, Vol I & II.* Hobby House Press, 1991, 1994.
———. *European Costumed Dolls.* Hobby House Press, 1994.
———. *Hard Plastic Dolls, I & II.* Hobby House Press, 1987, 1989.
———. *Glamour Dolls of the 1950s & 1960s.* Hobby House Press, 1988.
———. *Santa Dolls & Figurines.* Hobby House Press, 1992.
Langford, Paris. *Liddle Kiddles.* Collector Books, 1996.
Lewis, Kathy and Don. *Chatty Cathy Dolls.* Collector Books, 1994.
Mandeville, A. Glen. *Ginny, An American Toddler Doll.* Hobby House Press, 1994.
Mansell, Colette. *The Collector's Guide to British Dolls Since 1920.* Robert Hale, 1983.
Morris, Thomas G. *The Carnival Chalk Prize, I & II.* Prize Publishers, 1985, 1994.
Moyer, Patsy. *Doll Values.* Collector Books, 1997, 1998, 1999.
Niswonger, Jeanne D. *That Doll Ginny.* Cody Publishing, 1978.
———. *The Ginny Doll Family®,* 1996.
Olds, Patrick C. *The Barbie Years.* Collector Books, 1996.
Outwater, Myra Yellin. *Advertising Dolls.* Schiffer, 1998.
Pardella, Edward R. *Shirley Temple Dolls and Fashions.* Schiffer Publishing, 1992.
Perkins, Myla. *Black Dolls.* Collector Books, 1993.
———. *Black Dolls Book I.* Collector Books, 1995.
Robison, Joleen Ashman and Sellers, Kay. *Advertising Dolls.* Collector Books, 1992.
Schoonmaker, Patricia N. *Effanbee Dolls: The Formative Years, 1910 – 1929.* Hobby House Press, 1984.
———. *Patsy Doll Family Encyclopedia, Vol.1.* Hobby House Press, 1992.
———. *Patsy Doll Family Encyclopedia, Vol. II.* Hobby House Press, 1998.
Smith, Patricia R. *Madame Alexander Collector Dolls.* Collector Books, 1978.
———. *Modern Collector's Dolls, Series 1 – 8.* Collector Books.

Index

Schroeder's
ANTIQUES
Price Guide

. . . is the #1 best-selling antiques & collectibles value guide on the market today, and here's why . . .

Identification & Values of Over 50,000 Antiques & Collectibles

8½ x 11, 612 Pgs, $12.95

• *More than 450 advisors, well-known dealers, and top-notch collectors work together with our editors to bring you accurate information regarding pricing and identification.*

• *More than 45,000 items in almost 550 categories are listed along with hundreds of sharp original photos that illustrate not only the rare and unusual, but the common, popular collectibles as well.*

• *Each large close-up shot shows important details clearly. Every subject is represented with histories and background information, a feature not found in any of our competitors' publications.*

• *Our editors keep abreast of newly developing trends, often adding several new categories a year as the need arises.*

If it merits the interest of today's collector, you'll find it in *Schroeder's*. And you can feel confident that the information we publish is up to date and accurate. Our advisors thoroughly check each category to spot inconsistencies, listings that may not be entirely reflective of market dealings, and lines too vague to be of merit. Only the best of the lot remains for publication.

Without doubt, you'll find
SCHROEDER'S ANTIQUES PRICE GUIDE
the only one to buy for
reliable information and values.

COLLECTOR BOOKS
A Division of Schroeder Publishing Co., Inc.